The LADY,
Her LOVER,
and
Her LORD

The LADY, Her LOVER, and Her LORD

Bishop T. D. Jakes

Walker and Company
New York

First Large Print edition published in the United States of America in 1999 by Walker Publishing Company, Inc.

Published simultaneously in Canada by Fitzhenry and Whiteside, Markham, Ontario L3R 4T8.

Unless otherwise noted, Scripture quotations are from the King James Version of the Bible. Scripture quotations noted NKJ are from the New King James Version of the Bible. Copyright 1979, 1980, 1982, Thomas Nelson, Inc., Publishers. Scripture quotations noted NIV are from the Holy Bible, New International Version. Copyright 1973, 1978, 1984 by International Bible Society. Used by permission of Zondervan Publishing House. All rights reserved. Scripture quotations noted NAS are taken from the Holy Bible, New American Standard Version. Copyright The Lockman Foundation, 1960, 1962, 1963, 1968, 1971, 1972, 1973, 1975, 1977. Used by permission. Verses noted TLB are from The Living Bible. Copyright 1971. Used by permission of Tyndale House Publishers, Wheaton, Illinois 60189. All rights reserved.

Library of Congress Cataloging-in-Publication Data
    Jakes, T. D.
        The lady, her lover, and her Lord / T. D. Jakes.—1st large
    print ed.
            p.   cm.
        ISBN 0-8027-2736-0 (hardcover)
        1. Christian women—Religious life. 2. Christian women—
    Conduct of life. 3. Marriage—Religious aspects—Christianity. I. Title.
    [BV4527.J34   1998]
    248.8'43—dc21   99-17233
                                                                  CIP

Printed in the United States of America

10 9 8 7 6 5 4 3 2 1

To my wife—it has been such a joy to watch you evolve. The years have painted a grace on your face, a strength in your eyes, and an unmistakable elegance in your gait. You are more beautiful today than I have ever seen you. I didn't know when I married you how much of a treasure I was actually getting in one lace-clad, pearl-covered Nubian princess. You are the best deal I ever negotiated.

Every year I walk with God. He helps me to improve. He is making a good husband and father out of me. It has helped me so much to be specially crafted and designed for you. The pattern is perfect, but there are so many flaws in the material. Nevertheless, I am anointed to be your man, and I will walk with you wherever, whenever, however. Thanks for being my friend and lover, and for showing me the Lord in your undying insistence that I can do all things. Do not ever doubt that you are the strong gust of wind that I feel under me whenever I spread my wings. Because of you, I believe I can fly!

TDJ

Acknowledgments

There are a number of wonderful people who contributed in countless ways to my experiences in writing this book.

My gratitude to my family, who generously shared me with this manuscript. I will always appreciate your love and support. I also want to acknowledge the compassion and encouragement that I consistently received from my church family.

Thank you to Denise Stinson, my literary agent, Tom Winters, my attorney, and Kenneth Dupree, who helped me coordinate this project—your hard work and vision have significantly impacted this book and, consequently, my life. Your votes of confidence encouraged me and challenged me to delve more deeply into prayer.

Irene Prokop, although we never met, your early support and tenacity truly started the ball rolling.

Thank you, Joel Fotinos, for your enthusiasm and for introducing me to the Putnam family.

Everyone should have an editor like Denise Silvestro, who leaves me with no horror stories to tell.

Que English, your countless hours of careful typing added polish to my rather crude typing style. You are much appreciated.

Thanks also to A. Larry Ross and Associates, who helped to manage my schedule and protect my interests in countless ways.

Natalie Cole, your kind words of support mean a lot.

Finally, thank you to everyone at Putnam. You all treated me and my work with great dignity and integrity. My gratitude to Nanscy Neiman, Susan Petersen, Marilyn Ducksworth, Dan Harvey, Dick Heffernan, and everyone at JMS Marketing & Sales, Inc.

Contents

Introduction

When we consider that many homes receive their temperament from the mother, we see it's imperative that every woman recognize and nurture the unique gifts that she naturally possesses—the calm, sincere milk of an enriched heart, a sedate confidence, and an ability to gently influence those she loves. The mother may nurse at her breast. Her husband, her children, and even her career will be affected by her ability to pass on the very best of her to those she will influence. So I'm faced with the challenge of finding some parallel truth that will assist me in describing how crucial it is for every woman to find balance in her life and fulfillment in her heart. To what shall I liken the necessity of each woman being able to find a centered life that is not distorted or unfocused? Perhaps music is an apt metaphor, likely to penetrate the heart and affect the spirit of those women who desperately need to know this information. The men who are the lovers of these women will also benefit from these words, for it is the duty of every man to help his lady achieve her greatness.

Almost all people enjoy music in one form or another. We listen to and enjoy the chirping of birds and the humming of crickets. We turn on the radio and listen, and the music seems to distract us from the weary road we travel. Music brings a certain sense of well-being to us. Music consists of individual notes that are constructed for the purpose of producing harmonious pitch. If the notes are discordant, they sound like noise. It is when they are orchestrated into harmony that our souls rest in the tranquillity of gentle sounds. Life is very much like music. The art of living is to orchestrate and organize one's life in such a way that all of the various events and demands can be produced without their colliding into one another and creating noise. That is what we all want to achieve. But no orchestra can have harmony amid the diversity of its instrumentation if there is not a conductor to maintain timing and structure. The Lord is the conductor who orchestrates the affairs that tend to create the noise of stress in all of us. Without Him, life sounds like a junior high school band warming up for the march! The Lord brings calmness and order to a chaotic world. The tranquillity of contentment is the apex of existence. It does not matter whether you are wealthy or surrounded with the ragged furnishings of poverty, if you can attain contentment and inner harmony, you are as fulfilled as and perhaps more at peace than the richest person in the world. So take a moment to inhale a deep breath of air and exhale every stress you have ingested, and let's talk about turning the noise of your life into the music that you want to hear.

There are three areas that we want to bring into the perfect pitch of inner harmony. The woman has three relationships that must be balanced in order to achieve some semblance of fulfillment. The first is her relationship with herself, for a strong relationship with oneself is a necessary precursor to every other relationship in life. If a woman doesn't have a solid relationship with herself, she will recklessly pursue external relationships in the hopes of achieving internal peace. She will try to love others in a desperate need to find in them what she must find within herself. This pursuit will be futile and is the cancer that kills most marriages. She will do right things for wrong reasons and grapple with the disappointment that comes from expecting someone to give her what she must give herself. The lady will not be able to have healthy relationships with others because the weight of drawing from them things that she should get from within soon becomes too much for anyone to bear. Then the man becomes guilty over his inability to satisfy what is an insatiable need. He becomes reclusive and hides in the cave of his work, his excesses, and sadly may find himself led to infidelity, since the expectations of his other woman can be controlled by the excuse of his being married!

Marriage is a sacred relationship. It is the second important relationship in a woman's life. A woman doesn't necessarily have to be married to be happy, but there are few things that are as satisfying as the sweet nectar of true eros love and sharing your life with a partner who values and respects you. However, the woman who does not love herself becomes so thirsty for love that she rushes into love half-dressed and ill prepared. She will always love too quickly, hold too tightly, and more often than not, lose too quickly the one that she has aspired to grasp. She holds on to his every word like a child holding sand on the beach; she squeezes him tightly, but she opens her hand only to discover that he has slipped through her fingers, and she doesn't even know why he left.

But there is good news. There is a cure for the compulsive woman who loves too easily and then grieves for years over bad choices and denied gratification. If she relates well with herself and has a strong sense of self-worth, she can easily share her life with another person. She will not be prone to be bitter, defensive, or frantic, for she has a calm rhythm that keeps her in sync with her goals and in tune with those around her. Her life becomes a melody line that is captivating and pleasant to a man's ears. When he sees her, he wants to harmonize. If she chooses, it is a duet with balance and purpose. If she doesn't, she is a solo, perfect and effective even alone. If she is married, this woman will bring to the bed of her husband the soft petals of a rose that is free of thorns. He will not be pricked by loving her.

If she doesn't have a relationship with a man, she is now able to choose a husband who has a rhythm that is in harmony with her own. She has made good use of her time alone and has spent much time researching herself to better know what type of man will harmonize with her style of love.

Still, there is a third relationship that the aforementioned cannot replace. It is the base of the triangle. Many have attained great accomplishments in all other areas, only to find to their astonishment that something is missing. What's missing is the need for a relationship with the Lord. He provides the spiritual fortification that anchors the soul and becomes the foundation on which all else is able to rest. Inner strength and tenacity springs from the well of personal prayer. I am not talking about fleeing to a convent and draping yourself in a habit. Nor am I talking about fanaticism, which is often used as a smoke screen to hide frustration in other areas. But a pendulum swings only when it is attached and anchored to something that doesn't move. While people will change and you will change, it is nice to be fastened to something that is always the same. Anchor yourself in the Lord.

For I am the LORD, I do not change; . . .   Mal. 3:6(NKJ)

In the following pages, we will explore the various needs and functions of these three relationships. I am hoping that amid this general information you will find some elements that benefit you, and more important, that you will take the time to study your own behavior so you may put into practice the elements that are needed to become balanced.

It is not enough to feel like a woman. This book is written so that you might feel like a lady. If a woman feels like a lady and is able to celebrate herself, she will attract into her life people who reflect her own opinion of herself. There are moments when even the strongest woman can appreciate the reinforcement of a man who is comfortable with who he is and who can be her anchor in the storms of life. He will be the warm hand touching the small of her back, giving her the stability to go forward. He will give her the feeling of uncompromising love as she faces the various ages and stages of life. He gives her body release, her mind a melody, and her spirit a gust of wind that makes her able to soar. When the lady has a lover, her eyes sparkle, her smile is bright, and her voice is calm and passionate. With her lover at her side, her heart is peaceful, for she feels secure and can close her eyes and rest her head on his shoulder.

But, in the stillness of the night, when he has gone to sleep and there are pending issues on her mind, it is her Lord who works the night shift and watches over her in the dark. He is the one whom she can talk to when her words cannot describe what she is feeling. Her husband may understand what she says, but her Lord understands what she feels.

There are some things that the lady can receive only from within her. There are others that are a direct result of her having a warm arm wrapped around her on a cold night. But, when human hands fail, there is always the strength of the everlasting arms of God. We will explore how every woman can live a balanced life and attain success in each of these significant areas. We will share openly what it takes to maintain her identity, his attention, and the Lord's favor. Why settle for two sides of a triangle when you can have it all? The lady, her lover, and her Lord—let the three notes in your life sing in harmony. It's the sweetest song you'll ever hear.

Part One

The LADY

Chapter One

Falling in Love
with Yourself

Love—what a word! It is a small word possessing only four letters, but it is loaded to the brim with every imaginable feeling. The Greeks have many words to describe the multifaceted concept of love. They divide the *agape* kind of love from the *philia* kind of love. The *agape* describes the divine, while the *philia* describes the brotherly affection between siblings and shared among humans. They use the word "eros"—from which we get the word erotic—to describe the intimate love of a man and his wife. Love . . . what an intimidating feeling to describe accurately. It is limiting at best to be left with words alone to describe the abstract feelings of the heart, but to have only one word to describe all the types and levels of feelings, a word that means different things to different people—well, we often fail to describe the variety or the intensity of the intoxicating impact of the love feeling.

Love is to life what a scent is to a rose. It is the spice of life, and it adorns life as clouds decorate the skies. Many women have tasted the nectar of romance. Many men have swayed beneath the influence of the memory of a special moment shared with that special someone. Even the aged see youth rekindled in the emblazoned moments of affection and the displayed admission of concern. From the cooing sound of a contented baby, to the calm breathing of an aged grandmother, there is the constant need for and appreciation of affections that affect the ordinary and transform the mediocre. Yes, love is the magic elixir of the soul. It is a common denominator, something we all need regardless of our varied perspectives or vicissitudes of life. Whether love is communicated through a soft touch or a moistened eye, it is the message that we need. The method is immaterial in comparison to the magnitude of the message itself.

There is no drug that can compare with the intense, passionate feelings that are aflame when the heart is in love. It is love that causes the senses to heighten. It is love that causes the heart to pump honey to the soul and sedation to the mind. It is the sweet taste of the honeycomb that satisfies the taste buds of the soul. Without love, life tastes bland and success is empty.

What can compete with love? It has kept the sick man alive and made the well man feel sick. It is love that gives us courage and yet love that makes us afraid. It weakens the mighty and strengthens the feeble. It is the most intoxicating feeling that any of us will ever have the privilege of experiencing. If it is given to the worthy, it is reciprocated and fruitful. If it is invested on the empty opportunist, it can create a pain that nauseates the soul and afflicts the mind. It can make an average person seem extraordinary. It has the capabilities to alter our perceptions and heighten our vulnerability. It is love that made Christ die and still that same love that made him arise from the grave.

Without a doubt, we all want to experience love, but we must ask, Are we in love with others or are we in love with the idea of being in love? Many are the women, and men as well, who have turned to the arms of someone looking for the assurance that ultimately must come from within. How bitter they become when they look around for that which they must find inside themselves. They saddle their relationships down with undue weight and hold their partners in a perpetual state of guilt. They blame their partners for not being there for them. But what is actually meant is that their partners are not giving them what they expected. The greater question should be stated, Is it fair to expect anyone to bear the brunt of a life filled with pain and dysfunction? Who can restore what life has taken out of you, but God? Who can remind you of what God has promised you, but you? You are your own preacher, and occasionally you must say the kind of speech to yourself that enables you to be productive and accomplished.

There are many types of love. But the one that we must begin with is the tantalizing allurement of the impassioned heart that enables us to love others. It is that passion that must start at home before it goes abroad. For the greatest of human perceptions is when the heart can look into the mirror and smile at the image that is reflected therein. It is the grace that enables us to wink at ourselves and appreciate our own gifts. It is a healthy mind that can celebrate itself. Then and only then can we determine whether we are loving others because they are lovable or because we are so famished for love that we will settle for anyone or anything that gives to us what we should give to ourselves.

Light a candle, play a song, take a walk, and meditate on your own accomplishments. It is a poor hen that will not crow in her own nest. Quiet moments alone allow us to explore how deeply we are committed to our own sense of healthy well-being and fortitude. You must become the motivational speaker that is self-challenging. The passion to go forward is too important to be left to the happenstance of someone else's concerns for us. We need to be motivated, but it is dangerous to allow that need to become so overwhelming and desperate that it can only find fulfillment in the actions of someone else. We need to be self-motivated in order to survive.

Perhaps one of the most difficult things to achieve is the ability to be motivated by ourselves. Most of us have a tendency to live and receive motivation as martyrs. We live for others and their causes, making our own needs and presence secondary pursuits. Sadly, sometimes we place ourselves so far on the back burner that the dreams boil out and leave only a parched pot where once we had personal expectation. When dreams boil out, a scorching heat of stress and anxiety causes the kettle to give a shrill sound before the burning begins. That shrill sound can be heard in our excesses and overindulgences, which camouflage the fact that we are frustrated with dreams that are denied and hopes that seem deferred. The burning, destructive, compulsive behaviors could all be avoided if we only, with patience and perseverence, took life in small doses and allowed ourselves the privilege of having an appointment with our own attention and scheduled ourselves as clients that we must see before the day is over. In short, take time for yourself. Listen to the hissing sound before you catch fire!

It has been said that love is a many-splendored thing. If that is true, then one of those splendors should be directed inward. While we value and validate the worth of others, we must also take the time to fondly affirm our own sense of personhood and self-development. We must know that love is not an optional accessory that we can choose to exclude from life. It epitomizes the human experiences and celebrates all that we enjoy. It gives us distinction from lower forms of life whose presence is monitored by time alone. Our life is not the mere collection of days and months. We are connoisseurs of the fine architectural design of life, love, and the exchange of human energy. We are moved and motivated by the spirited synergy that comes from the passion of experiences and the fine nectar of moments shared.

The real challenge that we all have is to find a place of balance between martyrdom and narcissism. The art of avoiding extremes is an art that is drawn on the canvas of maturity and painted with the abstract strokes of many experiences. The balance is as vital to you as it is to a high-flying trapeze act. We need not become self-consumed, but please realize that there must be something between selfishness and self-denial. This is not the blaring clarion call to become self-centered and egotistic. But it is a cry to balance the heart of women who have allowed everyone's plight to become more important than their own. It is a cry to recognize your strengths before you become lost in a perpetual state of being a cheerleader for someone else and never yourself.

This is not just a feminine problem. It is actually a human problem. Yet the maternal instinct in women increases their susceptibility to it. Maternal instincts are great on a child, but don't try them on a man. They are dangerous when coupled with the societal bias that tends to usher women into roles of subservient behavior. It makes the lady a prime candidate to become a martyr for any cause but her own. When this happens, the milk of compassion in a woman often hardens in the breast and causes the heart to ache. There was nothing wrong with the milk. It was just invested in something or someone that was not worthy. There is nothing worse than giving the right thing to the wrong person.

Many women find it difficult to appreciate themselves because society puts pressure on them to be completely selfless; any attempt at self-nurturing and self-love is condemned, eliciting accusations of being selfish and narcissistic, of not being an adequate wife, mother, or even an adequate woman. No woman wants these labels and so many comply—giving, giving, giving—never appreciating themselves. Never realizing that in order to truly give you must appreciate the gifts you possess. Sadly, some women's lives become as futile as a child's attempt to capture the entire ocean in his sand bucket. No matter how committed he is to his task, no effort is ever enough.

It's not easy to overcome this pressure. Even the most liberated people are adversely affected by the pressure of public opinion. Withstanding the opinions of others is at best stressful and at worst debilitating. Many of us are crippled by those who do not allow us the freedom of our own opinions and the exploration of our own personhood. We all have a tendency to reflect the opinions of others. If someone says you look terrible in a dress, don't you wear it with reluctance the next time? Even though we say we do not care what people think, to some degree we are still vulnerable to their words and ideas. But if we are going to be effective individuals, we must develop the ability to embrace ourselves. A positive self-image is not arrogant. It is necessary in order to procure a healthy relationship with others. People who have low self-esteem are too obsessive to enjoy others. They cling to them like a vine to a wall. They need others to stand, and that need is compulsive and draining.

It is virtually impossible to find someone to appreciate you as a person if you do not allow them to see you as a settled, stabilized force in the earth. They need to hear you sing your own song. They need to listen to your solo. Sing the melody of success and everybody will want to hum that tune with you. But make sure that you allow to join in only those who harmonize with your own self-image. You actually train others how to treat you by how you treat yourself. Do not think for one moment that others do not observe your level of style, class, and preferences. All of us, when we shop, have had to deal with the fact that this person we are shopping for would or would not buy this item for him- or herself. You want to buy what would at least be comparable to what that person would select. You wouldn't give a cheap bag to someone who wears expensive clothes, would you? Who would feel comfortable giving a gift that would stand out among the person's possessions as an item beneath his or her normal standard? By being good to the self, this person has in essence set a standard that we all must aspire to reach if we are to be a blessing to that individual.

Look, Ma, No Hands

We are not born in relationships. Who among us was born holding someone else's hand firmly clasped within her own? We enter life with both hands up in the air and fists clenched tightly. We are born empty-handed. There are no hands to hold but our own. We learn to reach out, but only after we have had a chance to reach inward and upward. It is the upward reach of the spirit and the inward reach of the soul that enables the outward reach of the body.

Most of us are single-birth babies who spent time alone from the womb to the crib. We played in the crib alone. We learned the fundamental skills of entertaining ourselves. Alone is where we start and essentially it is where we end. For even if we die in a crowded room, ultimately we die alone. Job says he came here naked and returned naked. It is true. We find ourselves going full circle. We take no more with us than what we brought. We brought no one with us into this world, and even though we may hold hands as we die, still we face death alone. We are at best empty-handed travelers. We start with clutched hands, and we end with clutched hands. Between those two points, our hands will hold many things. But, at the end, as was in the beginning, they will pry our hands open and find no one's hand within but our own.

Nothing is more essential to spiritual and emotional well-being than that which we are considering now. For you see, there are some prerequisites to a healthy love relationship with others. We can love others with no more wholeness than that with which we love ourselves. We tend to seek from others the kind of love and affirmation that must come from within. As we journey forward, we will discuss the relationship the lady has with herself, then with her husband and lover, and finally with her Lord.

If her relationship is not fortified with her Lord and with herself, she will enter into a relationship with a man for the wrong reason. She will want from him those properties that can only be extracted from a positive self-image and a clear perception of her God. I will discuss in more detail later the significance of having a God-centered life. But for the moment, let's consider what can be achieved by a woman who knows and loves herself. So tonight, dear friend, set the table for one and sit in the presence of your own personhood. Drink the robust wine of your own thoughts and laugh hysterically at some humorous memory that you can share with no one but yourself. Could it be possible that before the night is over you might find yourself warmed by the fire of your own dreams, and perhaps ever so gently whisper the confession that by God's grace you have finally learned to enjoy your own company?

Could it be possible that being alone does not have to mean that you are lonely? Have you ever entertained yourself? Or are you saving all of your social skills for someone who is not there? If you are, it is indeed a statement that suggests you are not important enough to demand your own respect. That is a dangerous place from which to start life. Because if you cannot value your own existence and presence, you will eventually have trouble relating well to others.

Most people spend no time entertaining themselves. They only entertain others. They never plan an evening for themselves. They endure their time alone as if they had been exiled to solitary confinement. But it is the single woman who has the time to develop true spirituality. She is not encumbered with the concerns of children or mate. She has the time to strengthen herself on several different levels. She has the time to strengthen her economy, her spirituality, and her personality. Each area needs to be strengthened so that she can clearly discern, when offers come, whether she is in love or in need.

> An unmarried woman or virgin is concerned about the Lord's affairs: Her aim is to be devoted to the Lord in both body and spirit. But a married woman is concerned about the affairs of this world—how she can please her husband. I am saying this for your own good, not to restrict you, but that you may live in a right way in undivided devotion to the Lord.
>
> I Cor. 7:34–35 (NIV)

I am therefore suggesting that you have a relationship first with your God, secondly with yourself, and finally, out of the manifold fruits of your own habitation, you are ready to share with someone else what you have determined to be worth bringing to the table of love.

First things first. God is a God of order. He created Adam alone and then gave him a relationship. Adam had time with God and with himself before he had time with his lovely bride. If God has chosen to allow you a time of intimacy with Him, enjoy that Sabbath and receive it as an opportunity to savor your consecration and develop your qualities as an individual.

> Master, which is the great commandment in the law? Jesus said unto him, Thou shalt love the Lord thy God with all thy heart, and with all thy soul, and with all thy mind. This is the first and great commandment. And the second is like unto it, Thou shalt love thy neighbour as thyself.
>
> Matt. 22:36–39

Jesus says that the greatest commandments that are listed in the Word are thus: the greatest commandment is the one that demands that we love our Lord with all our hearts, minds, and souls; the second-greatest commandment is that we love our neighbors as we love ourselves. But how can we love our neighbors who are apart from us if we do not learn to love ourselves? It is here that we must begin the process of preparing our gift to be given. For how can we give to someone a gift that we do not value or believe to be significant ourselves? Is it possible that this is the basis for so many dysfunctional relationships? Is it possible that many people have a tendency to see themselves as insignificant and therefore open themselves up to a life of abuse?

More important is the fact that when we do not value ourselves, we tend to attract people who support that devalued image. Remember now, we train people how to treat us by how we treat ourselves. If you honor yourself, there are some men who will not find that an attractive feature. You will hear statements such as, "She thinks she is so much," or, "That girl is a trip." The truth of the matter is he has seen the product and doesn't have the price that the ticket says must be paid. You must know that sometimes rejection is a blessing and not a curse. There are some people, jobs, friends, and so on that you do not want to attract. You want to draw to yourself people who are comfortable with your values and perceptions. People with low self-esteem tend to draw to themselves others who dominate and control or belittle them. They attract the types of men who are apt to reinforce their own negativity. That is why you need to be healed inside before you enter into relationships.

Sometimes God delays relationships to give you a chance to heal as an individual. Then and only then can you make choices that are healthy—choices that are not predicated on obsessive need or fear of being alone. There are many people who endure unthinkable abuse because they are terribly afraid of being alone! To avoid themselves, they choose life with an abuser rather than a night at home alone. But there are some things that are worse than being alone.

While you are single, if you do not spend time finding wholeness and learning the art of being happy alone, you will marry out of fear and then years later awaken out of the comatose state of low self-esteem, only to recognize that you are a valuable entity whether there is a man around or not. Then you may find yourself lying beside someone who no longer fits where you are; he fit where you were and how you saw yourself before. You may find that you are tied to someone who fits your dysfunction but not your function. Tragically, you have grown apart rather than together. Many times, in response to the woman's new sense of value, the man will panic and try to insult the woman into a false feeling of incompetence. Women, do not embrace this degradation! Maintain the courage to disagree with debasement. There is a difference between constructive criticism and the killing of a human soul. Know that there is nothing damaged within you. It is the man who is insecure, devaluing you to compensate for his own weaknesses. A strong man's hands can clap for his woman and still feel good about himself.

Many brides walk down the aisle of the church secretly saying, "Save me, save me." It is the silent scream of a desperate heart that is in love with the idea of love, in love with the hope that someone will love her so well that she will finally feel good about herself. But before you make a tragic mistake, you must learn the art of being warm alone! Additionally, you must realize that this is the time during which you should develop a respect for your own opinions. This is not to say that the goal is inflexibility as it relates to others' opinions. No, we always want to be open to the wisdom others can offer. But it does mean you should have conviction in your own thoughts in the absence of all others and their advice. What do *you* think? Before you get a second opinion, be sure you have a first one. It is time alone that enables you to get a grip on your own feelings and develop your own reasoning. Take it from me, it is far better to fall in love with a whole woman who has her own opinions and creativity than it is to be married to someone who thinks only what *you* think and wants only what *you* want. On the surface, having a woman defer to you may sound noble to some men. But after a while, you want a woman who has an idea that you didn't give her!

In short, the melody must be established before the harmony can be written. You must first establish your own identity. Try to establish some solidarity financially, mentally, and spiritually. Then, when and if you add the harmonious thrust of a male counterpart, he is enriched by your contribution and you by his, without being a weight that he carries until he is exhausted. The goal is ultimately a state of wholeness. That wholeness cannot be reached if you are not divorced from your past and prepared for your future. So let's take it step by step, one day at a time, and watch God give you the grace to make changes and institute goals for your future.

Your assignment at this point is quite simple. You have three P's that you are to start with. They are prayer, praise, and pampering. Pray for strength because you know that He gives might to those who have none. Praise God for your survival because you know that it is by His mercy that you are still here. Pamper for solace. It is through pampering yourself that you find renewal and comfort against the tragedies of life. You could do all of these practices at the same time. Light a candle in the bathroom, play some soft notes, and slip into a hot tub with scented bath beads. Lie in the water and raise your hands in the air and praise the God that blessed you to be alive. Pray about the things that would normally worry you. Refuse to spend the evening worrying about things over which you have no control. Instead, lather up and relax—this is your time of pampering!

To everything there is a season, a time
for every purpose under heaven.

Eccles. 3:1 (NKJ)

Chapter Two

Female Footsteps on the Run!

The loving parents of little children look and muse as they see the wonder of new lives, filled with the promise of hope for the future. Yet as they look ahead with pride, they also want to protect their children from the inevitable challenges that come with maturity and achievement. Parents know the innocence of today can quickly be replaced by pain tomorrow, and tomorrow isn't that far away. I can still hear the sound of my daughter's tiny feet. They clapped the floor sounding like my grandmother's hands on Sunday morning. They sounded like the percussion section of a children's symphony, written in a cadence of laughter and often melancholy moods. The pitch varied from moment to moment, but the key was stable. My daughter was written in love, and for a little while, just a brief shining moment, she was written just for me.

But the clapping sound of bare feet is soon replaced by the sound of sharp heels and strong gaits. Daddy's little sweetie pie will soon be someone's sweetheart. She makes the steps that lead to womanhood one day at a time, and the steps between mud pies and quiche dishes are fraught with worry for parents. What a long walk the little feet must trod to reach pumps and pocketbooks. It is a long walk up a steep hill. The hill is so high that some do not make it without stumbling, suffering many bruises and scrapes along the way. What sane father doesn't fear what his daughter will face? What loving mother doesn't pray at night that her little girl will have a chance to fight? She must be a fighter, for sooner or later there will be a challenge for her to survive. She will not escape challenge. That is not likely. With quick steps, sure and sharp, she's stomping toward a destiny that no one can foretell. It is the uncertainty of the future that causes the heart of men to seek a God who can see where men's frail eyes are too weak to venture. Who can see tomorrow but the one who holds it in His hand? Today's girl is tomorrow's lady . . . maybe.

It is the sound of hurried footsteps that I hear racing toward womanhood and away from childhood. Baby, why do you walk so fast? Just a blink of my eyes, and you have gone from Pampers to puberty. I turn my head to hide a tear and look again, and you are gone into the arms of adulthood. But, at least for a moment, I get to listen to the clapping sound of bare feet on hardwood floors. Remember the wild look of wonderment that exists only in the eyes of little girls clad in lace frocks and shiny patent leather shoes. The bright eyes of promise and a hint of mischief are the only enhancements needed to a face that is already adorned with the cosmetics of youthful radiance.

Today's sound of soft feet and the sight of a tiny hand clutching a big doll fill our hearts with joy. See the little smile that trusts even strangers. Hear the sound of laughter so pure that it sounds like crystal-clear water rushing across rocks in the mountain's stream. It is a laughter that hasn't been touched, taught, or defiled. Today's little baby is a blank sheet of paper. What is written on her today will leave an almost indelible imprint behind.

If people understood that, they would not move so quickly, beat so easily, or touch so lewdly the lives of the little people whom we call children. They would carefully consider the things that they say or do. Sadly, most do not realize that thoughtless acts will leave our children scarred by painful memories and disrupted destinies. So adults, contemplate carefully before you make the first strokes on her little life. The lines etched in her childhood will draw the wrinkles of her old age. Be sure before the pencil touches that you are ready to write a permanent mark on the life of an innocent child. The mark you make today is the legacy that someone will live with for years and years to come.

As Little Children

Why do we love children? Even the most hardened of us has a certain tenderness for children. Could it be that there is hidden somewhere within us a simplicity that relates to the pureness within them? Isn't it true that we as adults spend our lives searching for the same thing that children do—that is, someone to be our friend? Somewhere, beneath all of our other goals, is the desire for someone to be our absolute, best, cross-your-heart-and-hope-to-die friend. Somewhere—before the divorces, scandals, spousal abuse, and manipulative marching band of relationships failed—lies a child who looks wide-eyed at strangers, hoping that each one is a possible friend who can be won.

What we call intimacy as adults is really allowing some other adult the privilege to see the child we hide in adult flesh. In their arms we curl into the fetal position and make soft sounds, dream pleasant thoughts, and wake as children stretching in the morning light. We do these things because beneath our adulthood and suave demeanor, we long for someone who can make us feel safe enough to be a child again.

Life is like a race in which all the participants are running feverishly to reach a destination. They run with exuberance and tenacity to attain some goal that seems to elude them. Yet each day they gird themselves like morning joggers and head out again for the racetrack of accomplishment, toiling madly to attain some level of success. This race doesn't start when we reach adulthood and enter the work world. No, this is a race that begins in the womb and at the count of three, with the grunt of a mother, we all come out running. Deep down, we all want the same thing, and we spend all our lives looking for it.

Layered below the tragedies and adversities that happen in life, there lies a hopeful dreamer who wants to find the answers to life before the questions are screamed in our ears. Life does have a way of screaming questions that demand answers immediately, and it seems as though it will punish us for not knowing the right answers. Almost every regret that you have now evolved when life presented the question and you lacked the answer. That is the real race to life: to know the answers before life asks the questions. It feels as though the art of life is to know your purpose and anchor into it before the bell rings, the class closes, and the night comes. Time is ticking, day is wasting, life is fading; we must learn in the light so we can choose in the night.

> I must work the works of him that sent
> me, while it is day: the night cometh,
> when no man can work.
>
> John 9:4

So how do we find those answers? I have dedicated my life to knowing three things. If I can die knowing these three things I will be listed with the sages of all ages. Number one, I must know myself. How can I love what I do not know, or mend what I have not seen? I must know myself. It is dangerous to allow others to know you better than you know yourself. Remember that knowledge is power!

Number two, I must know my source, my Creator. What does it profit to know the product if you have no relationship with the manufacturer? It is the relationship with the manufacturer that gives you comfort in a crisis. For when the product is in danger, it takes the manufacturer to redesign the technology or align the equipment. God is my manufacturer. I must know Him before I dare to know the third category. If I know the first two, I can study the third in relative safety.

Oh yes, number three. I must know my neighbor. I must know those who surround me. For even though we are born alone and die alone, we are not meant to live alone. We are social animals who need to love and care for others and have the same given unto us. I said you need to know yourself and your

Lord before you can enter into a true relationship, but a relationship is hollow if you don't really know the person with whom you're interacting. You can learn the dance steps and listen to the music, but if you don't know your partner's moves, you might as well be dancing alone.

I may have shocked you when I placed knowing myself as number one. But I did it because it is true. As children, we do not wake up in the morning wanting to know God as often as we are curious to know ourselves. Psychologists teach us that it is natural for a two-year-old to prod and touch his own body. He is not so much being sexual as he is on a journey of self-discovery. He glances in mirrors and touches all parts of his anatomy in the tub. He is curious about himself, first and foremost.

But it is the quest to discover the self that drives one into a need to know Him, for only through God can we know all that we are. One quest connects and directly relates to the other. We can't learn a word without knowing the alphabet, and we need to know all the words for a sentence to make sense. So too the way to the truth: we need to know ourselves, our Lord, and our neighbors for any of it to make sense.

If it takes my knowing God to know myself, then how can anyone talk to me for twenty minutes and walk away feeling like he knows me? It is unthinkable. It is an insult. It suggests that either he thinks himself that brilliant or he thinks me that shallow. Either is an indication that we are dealing with someone who walks on his toes or showers without turning on the water. It's ludicrous for anyone to think he can know me when I'm still studying myself. I do not know about others, but I am still doing lab tests on myself, discovering new facts each day. The results of every conversation are scrutinized, assessed, recorded, and filed. I am swimming in the petri dish of life's varied experiences, and I have not come up for air. Who could dare to think that he knows me just because he spent a few hours, a day, a week or two in my company?

How can you know the adult I am until you have touched the child I was? Do you not know that the decisions I make are based on the perceptions of the child that hides behind these weathered eyes? Perched behind an older frame lies a child who is still the same. It is that child who falls in love or feels hurt. It is the scampering of the child's feet who runs away from an abusive situation and then sits in the house and cries for weeks because I thought you were my friend. How could you marry me and not like me? It is the child who longs to go outside and play or snuggle up under a blanket. It is that child who must be reached if you are to know me at all.

> When Jesus saw this, he was indignant. He said to them, "Let the little children come to me, and do not hinder them, for the kingdom of God belongs to such as these." I tell you the truth, anyone who will not receive the kingdom of God like a little child will never enter it. And he took the children in his arms, put his hands on them and blessed them.
> Mark 10:14–16 (NIV)

No wonder Jesus said, "Suffer the little children to come unto me." He knew that a blessed child grows into a blessed adult. If we are going to come to Him at all we must come as a child or He will not receive us. That is who comes anyway. The little child within us is the one who comes to a God who is too far away to conceive calling him God, but who draws so much closer when we call him Father. The child in you needs to know your Father!

Jesus taught his disciples that unless you become as a little child, you will not inherit the kingdom. What you inherit is a direct result of whom you are related to. If you are related to evil, you can only inherit that with which you are surrounded. Children are the heirs of success or pain. They are the ones who are actually wrestling through their parents' divorce. They are often struggling long after their parents are remarried. Too often they are the heirs of their parents' mistakes. Why? Because injuries incurred early are far more lethal than those sustained later. It is when the sapling is young that it can be bent. We must bolster it early on so the tree can grow strong.

Chapter Three

Bent Babies Make Broken Ladies

Have you ever felt bent out of shape? There are some things that can happen to you that leave you disfigured. I do not mean outwardly, but inwardly. Many women in this country are bowed down under the weight and pressure that comes from deep, dark secrets and traumas that have left them twisted and misfigured. Issues, relationships, and incidents leap out of their past and hold them hostage, forever chained to emotional pain. Events of long ago permanently alter these women; the wounds might not be fresh, but the scars last a lifetime and never completely heal.

And, behold, there was a woman which had a spirit of infirmity eighteen years, and was bowed together, and could in no wise lift up herself.

Luke 13:11

The mangled heart of an abused woman looks much like a torn cloth doll. The fragile tissue of a tender little girl is torn into shreds that continue to unravel into her adult life. Soft, salty tears frequent the faces of women who have been through trauma too personal to be discussed and yet too evident to be hidden. They are haunted by memories of things they want to forget. It is not unusual for these women to wake in the night with a start. They weep at a movie—not because of the plot, but because they relate to the victim.

Understand that it is the bending of a sapling that makes the twisting of a tree. We see the tree with its mangled branches and mutilated trunk, but God sees the sapling that should have been left alone. It is nice to know that God is not like men. It is nice to know that God sees the sapling while men argue about the tree. It is the sapling that is twisted, and it is the sapling that cries in the night. It is the sapling that longs to be healed. You see, no matter how old the tree gets, it is still being affected by the sapling stage of life. We see the tree, but the Master knows that the tree is still wrestling with the misalignments of the sapling stage. Likewise, every man who ever held a woman, every minister who ever counseled an adult soon realizes that he is dealing with the results and influences of past experiences. It is not the clicking of black pumps that run toward human hands or divine words for help. It is the pitter-patter of little feet. Feet that were formed by adversity, challenge, and struggle.

We who minister to the broken hearts and lives of destitution and disappointment see a new thirst for spiritual awakening. We see grown women running to the altar, but the Father hears the sound of the pitter-patter of little feet. They are running to the altar. There is nowhere left to run. These are broken little girls grown taller but still bent over. They are filled with regrets and secrets, scars and traumas. They have to run from arm to arm, from man to man. They have run until they are tired of seeing the same things happen over and over again. To run without direction is like running rapidly in a circle. You spend a lot of energy, but you have so few results. It reminds me of walking for hours on a treadmill and finally getting off of it, tired and wet. The first thing you notice is that you have walked seven miles but you are still in the same spot. Have you ever looked back over your life and felt as though you have exhausted yourself traveling, but you still have not reached your destination?

Look down at your feet and wonder what they would say if they could speak. Where have they been, and from what have they run? These are the feet of America's children, grown larger but still aching. In fact, all over the world there is a mob of hurting people whose feet have run through fire rushing back home. They have tried to numb the pain through sin and did not win the peace that they sought. Now, since they have not been able to cry their pain to sleep, they run at last to Him. So run, little feet. The Father awaits you.

Stuck on the Steps

Sometimes, when the hurt becomes too much, it is easier to shut down. The sting of suffering cannot reach a heart encased in a hard, protective shell—but then, neither can love.

It is a state of emotional purgatory. When you block out the pain, you block all other feelings as well, and nothing, no one can touch you. Sermons don't touch you. Sex doesn't touch you. The lover's passionate caresses fail to touch the spot where it really hurts. Wild nights leave you empty. "Is something wrong?" they ask. "No, I am fine," you reply. But inside you ease out a sigh, turn in to a pillow, and feign sleep. They do not know that when they wrap their arms around you, they are not even holding you. The real you is cut off from the rest of the world. It's almost as if your heart were wrapped in a suit of armor. You are safe from pain, safe from anyone hurting you, but you are alone, empty, and untouched. You are making love, making life, making coffee, in a bubble. You are quarantined by pain and alienated by secret struggles. So close, but yet so far, you remain untouched!

This is loneliness at its zenith. True loneliness has little to do with whether you share a house with someone or a bed with someone. You can live with ten people and still be lonely. Loneliness is intensified when you have every reason not to be lonely, but you still are. Loneliness screams loudest when you are surrounded by people who are so close that you can feel their breath on your neck, but you are wrapped up in some invisible cloak. It isn't always that there is no one reaching after you. It may be that there are so many layers to unwrap that they are touching only the outer surface of the covering you have hidden in for years. What you built for protection has now become a prison, and you are trapped in a silent cell built for one.

I call it stuck on the steps! Shall we describe it as an elevator stuck between floors? To many, it feels as though something happened and life put them on hold, and they have been waiting for years for life to get back to them. The Bible says, "The steps of a good man are ordered by the Lord." But what if the feet get caught between steps? Have you ever felt stuck between ages and stages, faces and places? Are you hurting now over what happened then? Are there images that float around in your mind, voices from past conversations haunting you in the middle of the night? You're not schizo or strung out, just seeing your average run-of-the-mill ghosts. Unresolved issues. Do you find yourself arguing with people who aren't listening anymore? Many people who clamor for success do it to prove something to someone who isn't even there anymore. They are still involved with a ghost! A hurt woman is especially apt to entertain these mental hobos. They ride the train with her everywhere she goes. These are the faces that flash before her in the night. They are the playmates of the broken. They are the company of the wounded. They are the sad memories of lost chances and failed relationships. These are the bedfellows of the suffering. They are the demons that must be exorcised, the phantoms and ghosts that must be evicted from the heart of the one who would dare to look life in the face and say, "I will go on!"

That is what you must say if you are going to survive. You must look right into the flaming inferno of hellish situations and declare through parched, lonely, tearstained lips, "I will go on." Inside every victim there is harsh tenacity and steel will. Courage is born out of crises. Little girl, you have the power. It is in you through Christ. It is in you to succeed. No one succeeds without overcoming opposition. Wipe your face, strengthen your back, hold up your head, and survive!

No one can change their yesterdays, no matter how terrible they may have been. Update your life. This is now, not then. I pray for your courage to endure what you cannot change. Completely remodel the things that you can, and tell the rest of it to go play in traffic!

As I write this I am sitting by the ocean. It is where I always like to go when thoughts are flowing. It is here that I am most aware that I am finite. It is here that troubles diminish for me. As I watch the seagulls clamor at the wind, snatching bits of air beneath their wings, pushing themselves higher, and then riding on the momentum, I realize how many men have sat where I sit. They are dead, I am alive, and it is my turn to see what they saw.

The mighty ocean teaches us so much. It is where many songs have been written. It is where many lives have been lost. It is the place of battles and celebration, crises and conquest. Its rushing tides are not afraid nor intimidated. It just flows and brings to the shore those things that it chooses and hurls them at the land as if it were evicting certain objects and snatching others. Perhaps that is why the ocean has persevered so long. It knows how to release some things and grasp others. If you are going to survive, take a lesson from the ocean. Hurl some things away from you and bring oth-

ers to you, and when all else fails . . . just
go on.

Affect the Next Generation

Many daughters have done virtuously,
but thou excellest them all.
                                    Prov. 31:29

The challenge is to reach a place in
healing where you can discuss what was
once a silent frustration. When you can vent
it, that frustration turns to wisdom. It is at
the point that you reach outside of yourself and give to others that ministry comes
home to you.

I have noticed that when you are ad-
mitted into the hospital doctors now do not
keep you as long as they once did. They do
it for several reasons. Perhaps money and
insurance are factors. Also, there is generally such a shortage of beds that the moment you can safely do for yourself, they
release you to go home. It is at home that
you learn to get up and challenge your limitations. It is there that you, with careful
wisdom and compliance with instructions,
can finish the healing process. And it is there

that you can heal the spirit in the same way you heal the body.

There comes a point when you have received enough help that you are no longer on the critical list. The moment you can get up, it is good to do so. You gain strength by helping others. Tragically some people come to ministries only when they are on the getting end. The moment that they are recovered, they never give anything to the next patient. You will never become a minister as long as you lie in the hospital bed yourself. Get up and help someone else survive what you endured. There are so many people who need the bed you are in. You must give it to them and become a part of the solution instead of the problem. That, within itself, is a therapy.

Perhaps it is your lot to teach a class out of what was a calamity. Have you taught school yet? God takes the broken and the wounded and rehabilitates them so that they can be clinicians of healing and instruments of life. You want to know what to do with your life. You are stuck on the steps in a job that is not fulfilling, and you are getting older and want to do something that matters to you. Fulfillment is not always a matter of income. It means a lot when you can lie down at night and know that what you did today made a difference in someone's life. I tell you now that your ministry is where your misery has been. That same spot that made you cry and moan is where you can bring honor and healing to those who are touched with the same pain. That is the spot where your compassion will skyrocket, and you can help the next generation of victims to get out of their beds and walk.

> And that He might make known the riches of His glory on the vessels of mercy, which He had prepared beforehand for glory . . .
>
> Rom. 9:23 (NKJ)

The Scriptures call them vessels of mercy. They are merciful because they have needed mercy. These former patients have a compassion that comes only from having been in the bed themselves. Their mercy is rooted in memories of their own tragedies. If you have ever endured a storm, you have such a different attitude from people who have never suffered or failed. You have become a vessel of mercy and God wants to use you. You should teach the next generation how to avoid the school of hard knocks. Wouldn't it be nice to teach your daughters, so that they don't have to face what you did, to know what you know? You know things that can save them from storms, tears, and traumas. If you cannot save them, you can at least coach them through it. After all, you've been there, done that. Teach them. Speak up loud and clear. It is urgent that we break the cycle of going through the same pains from generation to generation. Stop the madness and save the sound of little feet. The sound of little feet is almost extinct today. Where are all the children? Hasn't anyone noticed that there are no chalk marks on the sidewalks? Hasn't anyone noticed that there are no Hula Hoops being sold? What has happened to the pitter-patter of little feet? Where are the little girls I used to know? Where are the little girls with shy stares and quaint attitudes, adorned with bobby socks and barrettes? Why are the girls who once were riding tricycles now pushing baby carriages? We have lost the sound of childhood.

I can feel the squirming of the little bodies of children who are smothered by vulgarity, exposed to pornography, and robbed of a childhood. Little girls are left home alone and the enemy is smiling like a greedy pimp

46

waiting on the next crop of fresh meat. He doesn't have to use drunk uncles to commit incest anymore, he is using day-care workers and baby-sitters, pedophilic priests and computer chat lines. These little ones who have been assaulted and molested by the age of ten and twelve are not even allowed to discuss their pain.

Some have not been molested; they have been spectators, but victims just the same. They were eyewitnesses to the most heinous acts of cruelty that the world has ever seen. These are the children who saw crimes acted out in the home. Crimes where the victim and the perpetrator were both related to the little witness. Their homes were as vicious as any battleground in the world. They grew up hidden in the closets of homes filled with domestic violence. They woke to the sound of shattering glass and cursing insults. Their ears were filled with the rape and assaults of their own mothers. They heard the muffled sound of beatings, the cracking of belts, the squeaking of box springs, and smothered screams for help. They were not the direct victims, just the witnesses of a nightmare from which they cannot wake up. They are the sad casualties of a cold war. A war that we are losing.

This is the twisted mutilation of tender minds. It is the gut wrenching, mind rending, heart breaking of children whose memories should be filled with baking bread and warm mittens. But instead they are filled with the mental nausea of half-digested events that keep their minds regurgitating and their hearts sick with thoughts that will not go away. It is the twilight zone of the adolescent heart. Their puberty becomes mangled in the meshing of adult issues and childhood thoughts. The outcome is a cocktail of pain and a lifetime of debauchery.

Some of you know that I am telling the truth. For only your eyes hide the secrets of your own pain. You who were exposed to too much too fast are living witnesses that you don't have to die to go to hell. The heat of your past has threatened your future with its blazing inferno of memories and side effects that still haunt you. There are issues in your past that may still be affecting you today. They collect on you like vapors on a mirror after a hot shower. The shower is over but the steam lingers. These are the loitering images that haunt the minds of adults. These scars lie around our hearts like phantoms, appearing and disappearing vapors of life's tempest. Have you anything left lin-

48

gering that needs to be wiped away? I would like to tell you that God has the ability to wipe away what neither sex nor drugs, wine nor money can erase. None of these unsavory solutions has the ability to heal the trauma. They only numb us for a while but then leave us bitter, angry, or depressed— by-products of our inner agony. But my God is the mender of broken dolls. He stitches together with skilled hands the dreams that have been ripped apart, the hopes that have been torn asunder. If your life lies tattered like an aged doll cast in the corner of a dilapidated attic, I would recommend Him to you. Come running to Him, and let Him fix your battered soul that has left you lying wilted on the floor.

Have you ever seen a broken woman? You cannot tell her by her clothes or hair. Nor can you describe her by her race or the number of degrees she has obtained from a university. Look for the slight traces of scars beneath her makeup, a blank, dead stare that neither eye liner nor shadow can give life to. Look for a smile that fades too quickly or a pained glance that stares into a past too hideous to be described and too heinous to be forgotten. Have you ever seen the empty gaze in the eyes of one who has seen hell's fire and been scorched by a story that she has no courage to tell? She often hides her helplessness in anger. She wraps herself in bitterness. It seems the only protection she can muster on her own. She is similar to a tame animal playing savage, hoping no one will know that beneath her growl there are no teeth, just tears. There are hot, blazing tears that come out at night like owls and hang perched on her eyelids, silently glazing her face till morning when she must put on her mask again and go out to work. She is a vase that has been cracked, leaking life, losing love. She has trouble maintaining relationships. It seems relationships slip through her fingers like sand held too tightly.

Jesus answered and said unto her, Whosoever drinketh of this water shall thirst again: But whosoever drinketh of the water that I shall give him shall never thirst; but the water that I shall give him shall be in him a well of water springing up into everlasting life. The woman saith unto him, Sir, give me this water, that I thirst not, neither come hither to draw. Jesus saith unto her, Go, call thy husband, and come hither. The woman answered and said, I have no husband. Jesus said unto her, Thou hast well said, I have no husband: For thou hast had five husbands; and he whom thou now hast is not thy husband: in that saidst thou truly. The woman saith unto him, Sir, I perceive that thou art a prophet. Our fathers worshipped in this mountain; and ye say, that in Jerusalem is the place where men ought to worship. Jesus saith unto her, Woman, believe me, the hour cometh, when ye shall neither in this mountain, nor yet at Jerusalem, worship the Father. Ye worship ye know not what: we know what we worship: for salvation is of the Jews. But the hour cometh, and now is, when the true worshippers shall worship the Father in spirit and in truth: for the Father seeketh such to worship him. God is a Spirit: and they that worship him must worship him in spirit and in truth. The woman saith unto him, I know that Messias cometh, which is called Christ: when he is come, he will tell us all things. Jesus saith unto her, I that speak unto thee am he.

John 4:13–26

Broken women find it difficult to maintain relationships. They are always looking for someone who can carry the weight of their pain. The only man I know who is attracted to carrying others' pain is Jesus. All others give out, get tired, and run out. Too much weight broke the wagon. If you put too much weight on humans, they will fail you. No one is attracted to a problem except a problem solver. His name is Jesus, and he has got your number! Any other man is looking for a whole woman. I know it is ironic, but even the broken man wants a whole woman. He wants something from her that he does not possess himself. Ah, the double standards of love are so unfair, yet it is true. He is looking for a woman who is able to contribute to his life.

Often a broken woman is entering into the relationship looking for someone to save her. Or at least someone to prove to her that he is not like the rest of the men in her past who have done her wrong. Who wants to start a relationship competing with all of those ghosts? A man wants to have a relationship with you, not your old boyfriends. Before you have another broken relationship, please take a minute, stop by the well, and let Jesus Christ rid you of those ghosts! Otherwise you will find it difficult to find anyone who will fill your void.

Jesus met such a woman at the well. She had multiple relationships, and she was involved in an affair when he met her. Now, Jesus could have rightly chastised the men in her life for using her, abusing her, robbing her of her dignity. But he goes beyond the blaming stage, which never brings healing anyway, and questions the woman about her inner thirst. He didn't waste time attacking the opportunistic suitors who had attached themselves to her life as locusts to a wheat field. No, he knew that they were the symptom, but she was the problem. He knew that beneath her varied affairs and relationships, she was a broken, thirsty woman who was desperate for a drink that would satisfy her. Not satisfy her flesh, but her soul. He identifies her problem as a thirst that only He could quench. If you are losing life and leaking love, you need to allow Christ to heal the broken pieces of your heart. He can then give you water so that you thirst not. Wouldn't it be great to enter into a relationship without being so thirsty for love that you couldn't trust your own discernment? When you are not so thirsty for love, you can make better decisions.

All Dressed Up and Nowhere to Go

Many women can get dressed up and display themselves gracefully as exquisite pieces of fine china, but underneath they secretly feel unclean. This is the pain that showers will not wash away, soap will not clean, nor cosmetics hide. It is the shrill scream of an anguished soul that cannot be heard by even those closest to them. But God hears the wailing of the muted voice. He hears the faint groan that seeps out in the night, like leaking sewage from a broken pipe. It is a mystery to most men, but it is the key that is necessary to understanding so the healing can begin. You can know the woman you hold, only when you have touched the child she was. It is the little girl who holds captive the silent woman. Heal the child with the word of God, and the woman will be free.

My sister used to dress up in my mother's clothes. I guess that wasn't so strange. Most girls make believe that they are all grown up. They spend time in the mirror making up their faces and brushing their hair, acting as though they are sophisticated socialites. It is just a game, a game to pass the time while Mother is away shopping. But for the nearly twenty-five percent of girls who have been molested and abused at early ages, make-believe isn't fun anymore. Someone walks in and turns make-believe into reality. An adult may touch the girl as if she were a woman, leaving behind a bent sapling that will grow into a twisted tree. In the snap of a finger, a brutal rape, a drunken wife-abusing husband, or a forbidden touch by a respected uncle can alter a girl permanently. All those days of playing grown-up, and one senseless act of abuse has stolen her youth forever.

Isn't it amazing that the only thing that separates the distinguished, well-adjusted high achiever from the substance-abusing, prescription drug–addicted, promiscuous girl of no standards is an event that can take place in a few minutes? I know that there are exceptions, but I have found that many of the broken people in our society are the results of tragic secrets. This harsh truth may make us troubled. It makes us uncomfortable to admit that there but for the grace of God go I. A few minutes left alone, and you would not be who you are or what you are in the way that you are. That is how close we are together on this planet: we are separated only by incidents and accidents that we encounter along the way. A few minutes is how close you were to not being defined as you are right now. A few minutes, and poof, your dreams have turned to ashes and your head lies twisted, your doll is broken, your hymen torn, and now you are a statistic. No, not a statistic, because in order to be a statistic you have to tell. Shhhh, this is a group that never talks or tells.

For these little ladies "make-believe" isn't fun anymore. They are forced to play adult games of the most horrid kind. They are too old to go back to their playmates and feel like a child, but too young to fit in with women. They are stuck between the steps. They are the forgotten generation. They are executives and maids. They are black and white. They are attractive and plain. They are overweight and anorexic. They are promiscuous and frigid. The symptoms are different, but the pain is the same. They come in all colors and classes. Take your pick—they are all around you.

Pain Is Driving a Porsche

But what things were gain to me, these I have counted loss for Christ.

56

> Yet indeed I also count all things loss
> for the excellence of the knowledge
> of Christ Jesus my Lord, for whom I
> have suffered the loss of all things,
> and count them as rubbish, that I may
> gain Christ.   Phil. 3:7–8 (NKJ)

We permit pain to hide behind money. We let it hide because in this country we believe that success cures pain. We do not minister to the wealthy, only to the homeless. We should help the poor, but we cannot stop with them. You don't have to be poor to be broken. There are many people who are sitting in a hot tub contemplating suicide. There are many famous, wealthy people who never hear about Christ. Christ is not just the God of the welfare mother. He is the God of everyone—rich and poor alike. And pain reaches all social classes. Pro football players, models, actors, and chief executive officers are at their wits' end. They are stressed and empty, hurting and vulnerable. It cost them so much to get what they have that they have nothing left to maintain where they are. Yes, pain is driving a Porsche today. It isn't just pushing a broom. Pain belongs to the country club and owns a set of golf clubs. It owns its own company.

If you were raised to think that all you had to do to be happy was marry money or finish school and move to the east side of town, I have a news flash. Suicide is on the upswing among professionals, and divorce is highest where there is something to be gained in the settlement. Pain doesn't just confine itself to the projects. It is alive and well in Beverly Hills. Why do we need to know that the one thing left in this country that is completely unprejudiced is pain? We need to know it so that there is no need to worship success, accomplishment, wealth, or influence.

Ask Lydia, who was an affluent, successful businesswoman. She was a beautiful woman, who sold dyes and dyed goods from as far away as Thyatira. She had her wealth but was not fulfilled. In Acts 16:12–15,40, she heard Paul preach, and she was converted. When she heard Paul's ministry, she suddenly realized that she needed Christ to complete her faith. She realized that God blessed her to be a blessing to the lives of others. Her resources and contacts were available for the ministry. She became a completed woman, and she was used by God in a mighty way. Eventually you want to do something with what you have acquired or it is a meaningless pursuit. Financial empowerment without purpose does not add up to fulfillment.

If someone had looked at Lydia's outward wealth and failed to recognize her inward poverty, they would have robbed her of an opportunity to be a completed woman. There are thousands of Lydias in this country. They have climbed the ladder to success and found that there is little fulfillment on the top rung. They need to know about Jesus and his love. Do you understand that this message is for the affluent as well as the impoverished? There are a whole lot of different types of brokenness. They do not always focus on being impoverished. There are those among us who have not been ministered to because our society suggests that when you are famous or affluent you must be fulfilled. But ask Lydia, whose life was so changed that she became a major supporter of ministry. She represents not only God's ability to heal the affluent, but she also dispels the stereotype that Christianity is oppressive to women. To the contrary, it is the emancipator of intelligence and the liberator of excellence. Lydia is a role model for women who aspire to excellence!

On the Sabbath we went outside the city gate to the river, where we expected to find a place of prayer. We sat down and began to speak to the women who had gathered there. One of those listening was a woman named Lydia, a dealer in purple cloth from the city of Thyatira, who was a worshiper of God. The Lord opened her heart to respond to Paul's message. When she and the members of her household were baptized, she invited us to her home. "If you consider me a believer in the Lord," she said, "come and stay at my house." And she persuaded us.

Acts 16:13–15 (NIV)

God stepped into Lydia's house that day and healed everything in her home. He did what none of her finances could do. He spoke peace to her home and deliverance to her family. Please hear this word, and realize that there is a reason that God has sent this ministry to you. It is time for you to open your home to the Holy Spirit and allow Him to work in your life. He is waiting for a chance to speak healing words to the wounds that have infected every area of your life. If you have everything but Jesus, you have nothing at all.

Pain is an equal-opportunity problem. It attacks the rich and the poor. Immediately after Paul left Lydia's house he met a slave girl, a fortune-teller, and he ministered to her.

> And then it came to pass, as we went to prayer, a certain damsel possessed with a spirit of divination met us, which brought her masters much gains by soothsaying. The same followed Paul and us, and cried, saying, These men are servants of the most high God, which shew unto us the way to salvation. And this did she many days. But Paul, being grieved, turned and said to the spirit, I command thee in the name of Jesus Christ to come out of her. And he came out that same hour.
>
> Acts 16:16–18

In one brief interval, the gospel has reached this businesswoman and then transcended culture and affluence by touching a slave girl. Perhaps that old hymn of the church says it best:

The blood that Jesus shed for me
Way back on Calvary
The Blood that gives me strength
From Day to Day
It will never lose its power.
The old song says
It reaches to the highest mountain
And It flows to the lowest valley.

If Lydia is the highest mountain among women, this slave girl is the lowest valley. She was poor and a slave. She was involved in the occult, and she was under the control of evil influences. But when she heard about Jesus, he delivered her completely. I can think of no instance any more graphic in terms of depicting the height, the depth, and the length of God's love. He can reach from one extreme all the way to the other. There is no difference in the price of redemption required for the affluent than for the impoverished. The same blood that washes the witch cleanses the businesswoman. Have you allowed that soul-cleansing, mind-renewing, efficacious blood to cleanse you? It doesn't matter whether your background is more like Lydia's or if you have been dabbling in the occult. He has the power to break through the darkness with his precious light!

Although your past may be laced with tragedy and filled with pain, God still offers the balm that heals. He erases the scarred and bleeding residue that attests to the horrors you have incurred. He is there to show you how to maximize on the maladies of yesterday. Take those traumas and tragedies, and turn them around. No matter what you've been through, remember you're still here. You're a survivor, and some little girl needs to know your recipe for survival. She doesn't need to hear about your successes; she needs to hear about your failures. Somewhere in the streets, there is someone dying because they do not know that it is possible to live through what you have already endured. You are a precious commodity. You are the cure to the crises. I know you say, "How can I be the cure when I myself am hurting?" Look at Jesus. He was giving life when he was dying. He healed the pained because of his pain. He was wounded for our transgressions. Could it be that you went through all you have so that you could help someone else?

There is no way to alter the past, but there is a way to benefit from it. Recently, my wife's mother died. Her mother was such a strength to us both that we were devastated at her loss. I told my wife, from my own experience with pain, that the hurt does not go away. It lightens, but it never vanishes totally. I said to her that the only way to vindicate the death of a parent is to give to your children what you didn't get yourself. To offer away what you want is a principle of Scripture. The thing that you need the most is the thing that you give. It will come back to you multiplied.

> Give, and it shall be given unto you; good measure, pressed down, and shaken together, and running over, shall men give into your bosom. For with the same measure that ye mete withal it shall be measured to you again.   Luke 6:38

You may be hurting now, but the best remedy is to give the comfort you never received. The wisdom of your experiences is a gift you can share, and as you lighten the load of others, you lighten your own. Ask the Lord for strength so you may give unto others the strength to survive. And through your own ministry, you will be healed.

A Prayer for Someone Who Needs It Right Now

Father,
I admit that I am hurting today. I know that I have been through pain, and I realize that all of it has not totally been recovered. Yet, I know that there are those that are worse off than me. Give me an opportunity to give encouragement out of my wisdom. As I give to others what I wish someone would give to me, I thank you for replenishing me and giving me living water. I confess my life is filled with stagnant water. All that has not leaked out of me is not moving forward, but today, O God, I stir up my waters. I am through just shedding tears of depression. I thank you for blessing me as I give to those who have need. Someone else needs this bed more than I. Now, Devil, you have held me in this bed long enough. In the name of Jesus, I will arise and be healed!
Amen

Talk to the doctor, and he will tell you that the inoculation is made from the infection. The antidote is made from the venom. That same principle is true about ministering to people. The best people to help others are not those who studied life in a book. It is those who lived it. You will never be healed until you use your pain to heal someone else. Ministry gives purpose to pain. It widens the gulf between then and now and announces to the perpetrator, I am healed.

> Brethren, I do not regard myself as having laid hold of [it] yet; but one thing [I do] forgetting what [lies] behind and reaching forward to what [lies] ahead, I press on toward the goal for the prize of the upward call of God in Christ Jesus.
>
> Phil. 3:13–14 (NAS)

It lies behind you, so bury it. Pronounce last rites over it. You have the authority to release the past in the name of the Lord, and today you must move on to what lies ahead! It is knowing when pain is dead that liberates us to help others with the testimony of it. The testimony is what you have left when the test is over. Commit the past to the ground. Throw the dirt of helping others on it, and it will die before your eyes. Somebody needs you right now. This is an emergency. Stop feeling sorry for yourself, and get involved. On the other side of your silence there is a fountain that quenches the wounded souls of broken humanity. You may not choose to share details. It is just important that you help others who are struggling with what you have survived. Maybe if you reach the children, we can again hear the sound of little feet, safe and sound, strong and staid. I miss the sound of little feet, whole children, happy homes, and family outings, don't you?

Chapter Four

The Grace to Be a Lady and the Strength to Endure

Who can find a virtuous woman? for her price is far above rubies.

Prov. 31:10

The Hebrew word that is translated as "virtuous" is *chayil*. *The New American Standard Bible* translates *chayil* as excellence, while *The Brown Driver Brigg's* definition uses terms like "strength," "ability," "efficiency," and "force." *Chayil* is what God calls a woman who has her act together. "She is 'chayil,'" says the writer who pens the description in Proverbs 31:10 that becomes the epitome of defining Christian virtue in feminine form. This woman is a star. She is an absolute ten! She is simply chic. No, better yet, she is *chayil*! She is full of strength and wisdom, she has the force of an army!

These are not the words that are used to draw a picture of a prudish, weak girl who has no ambitions or goals. This is a woman who is progressive, resourceful, and yet as we delve into her she is incredibly balanced. Balance—it is the hardest thing to attain but the most necessary ingredient when aspiring for success. To be balanced is to have and maintain all elements in their proper proportion. All parts of your life, all aspects of your personality, need to be fully developed. If one area is deficient or exaggerated, you will be imbalanced. Leaning too far toward one thing or veering too far from another will sooner or later make you tip over. Instead, endeavor to pay attention to every aspect in equal measure, and you will be balanced.

Shouldn't this be a goal for every woman, and every man for that matter? Is it your goal? It should be, if you hope to be a woman of excellence. You might think that a woman of excellence would have to be someone who has been exposed to all of the social advantages of breeding and class. You might imagine her to have sat attentively in ballets and hosted countless afternoon teas for various prestigious charitable foundations. You might think that she would be required to recite poetry and extend her pinkie when sipping exotic tea from eggshell china. But we are not merely talking about the societal definitions of excellence. Nor are we buying into images that do not necessarily depict internal qualities such as strength and fortitude.

Excellence is an ambition, not a pedigree. It's about the woman's destiny, not her origin. Excellence speaks to her self-perception and the standards that she will not deviate from. It draws a line in the sand and says, "Nothing less than this will do in my life anymore!" A woman of excellence knows what she deserves and will work tirelessly to attain it. Do not be discouraged if you have failed or fallen in the past. Excellence is not based on past performance. It is a title given to someone who persisted and rose above her calamities.

A woman of excellence is armed with a road map that is marked, and her destination has been set. This woman has a blueprint for living. She is not wandering aimlessly and hoping to be found by someone. She is driving on what some call the road less traveled—a road only the great will travel. And she knows exactly where she wants to go. She has a certain something about her. Some will call it arrogance; others will smirk and suggest that she has forgotten wherefrom she came. Boy, are they mistaken. It is the memory of where she was that gives her the strength to arise and keep driving.

A woman of excellence is like a thoroughbred, graceful and strong, a creature of rare beauty. She is a winner. She is a diamond that has started as coal but turned into a jewel. She is as rich in class as white wine served in a chilled, gold-stemmed goblet, whirled around and then sniffed before tasting. She is an exquisite wonder that this generation seldom beholds. What can I say? She is simply a lady.

The lady is an endangered species. Like the gentleman, her masculine counterpart, she is almost extinct. There is more to being a gentleman than being a male. Likewise, there is more to being a lady than being a female. A real lady is unique and valuable. The breeding required to produce her has been deemed outmoded and irrelevant. She has been replaced by a more modern, less caring, poorly crafted, carelessly calibrated, and a crassly competitive caricature. A lady is a sensitive, temperate, competent woman who has ambitions yet possesses class and finesse. She is a woman with a dream. She is the pristine prima donna of days gone by. She is sadly missed.

I know when we start talking about elegance and using terms like pristine, you associate it with male dominance and the historical oppression of women. Admittedly, women were not always treated justly. Men often took unfair advantage of their dainty demeanor and chaste disposition. However, it is the action of the man that needs mending, not the woman. We must be like the florist who strips the rose of its thorns but leaves its petals. Is there no way to clip the prickly parts of life and maintain the fragrant?

When we search for the woman of excellence, there is one thing we must consider: the possibility that she has drowned in the rebellion that is so characteristic of an abused, neglected, unappreciated species. The glory days of yesteryear were filled with gender bias and injustice. Unfortunately, the good ole boys' club is still up and running. Woman has suffered immeasurable abuse and mistreatment, and in response, she has had to become a fighter, hardened to the world that has done her wrong. Yet beneath the mask or hard exterior, there is a soft center that she hides from public view. She is afraid for it to be seen. The last time she showed it to someone, she was hurt, and so she thrives and progresses by smothering her femininity and burying her compassion.

I know why the lady is missing, but oh God, she is missed nonetheless. I know her disappearance was an act of defiance and perhaps frustration. I know what oppression can do. My generation was filled with revolutions. We were going to change the world. I can remember all the hippies who were driving yellow Volkswagens with the peace sign on the bumper. The women burned their bras. The guys stopped wearing underwear. And free love and harmony with the planets were the messages of the moment. Somehow after the Vietnam War, we discovered that the VW was now rusted, the blue jeans started chafing our groin, and we were more interested in landing on the moon than grooving with the planets. Suddenly we heard it through the grapevine that we needed r-e-s-p-e-c-t. The Jacksons were no longer five. The Beatles broke up, the stock market went

74

up, and soon O.J. meant more to America than orange juice. Meanwhile, the interest rate accelerated, Jimi Hendrix had deflated, and alas, Elvis really had left the building.

Those were the days, my friend—what a challenging age for us to live in. Reality began to set in, and we began to settle down. We needed a job, breasts needed a bra, and we realized that maybe civil rights wouldn't be straightened out at the next march. Women began to redefine themselves while men went into some unisex oblivion, and now we are somewhere in the twilight zone of divorce and teenage pregnancy. Now, amid the mess we created, we are finally looking for the return of old-fashioned values. We want the rose of simpler times. Can we have it? I am not sure. But we must try to recapture the fragrance from the rose without being pricked by the thorns.

Many have felt the earth move under their feet, and when it finally stopped moving, they had been changed forever. Some had been married and divorced. Some had been raped and rejected. The earthquakes of life have done a lot of damage. But we are survivors, and now we realize what our parents knew thirty years ago. Unfortunately, by the time you figure out the plot of life, the movie is almost over and the credits will soon run across the screen. Who would have ever thought that the whiz kids of the seventies would be parents with streaks of gray? We are running out of time.

No time for games now. It is too late in the day. You can suppress who you are but you cannot change who you are. You were created to be the softer shade of blue. Many of you are depressed right now because there is another woman inside of you screaming, wailing, "Let me out!" She is tired of dressing up in "I don't care" clothes! The softness that our generation seems to want to bury must be liberated. In spite of the pained past. You must open your heart or you will suffocate your creativity, stifle your feelings, and diminish the brief moments of life you have by living in a vacuum for fear of pain.

Vacancy: Apply Inside

So the LORD God caused a deep sleep to fall upon the man, and he slept; then He took one of his ribs, and closed up the flesh at that place. And the LORD God fashioned into a woman the rib which He had taken from the man, and brought her to the man. And the man said, "This is now bone of my bones, and flesh of my flesh: she shall be called Woman, because she was taken out of Man."

Gen. 2:21–23 (NAS)

Man was created with the woman hidden in his being. God then skillfully brings out of him that hidden part called woman. She was taken "out of him." Her removal left a void and this creates man's attraction for her. She was the softer side of him. She was his tenderness, and those emotions he couldn't share. She was the tears that would not fall, the passion he didn't allow himself to feel, and the trembling compassion that he could never express. When he makes love to her, he is actually embracing the softer side of himself. He is holding all that he is unable to say in his arms and loving it, touching it, stroking the part of his being that wishes it could be held, and if he is wise, he does it with all his strength. Tenderness, sensuality, and passion erupt when he has the knowledge that he is somehow making love to the softer side of himself.

So husbands ought also to love their own wives as their own bodies. He who loves his own wife loves himself; for no one ever hated his own flesh, but nourishes and cherishes it, just as Christ also [does] the church . . .

Eph. 5:28–29 (NAS)

No man gets a relief from holding a woman who exhibits the same characteristics he already has. In fact, his very attraction for her is predicated upon the part of him that is missing. She is the missing rib that left his side hollow. When he connects with her, he feels somehow complete. She was not created man. God already had one of them. She is the many-splendored, multifaceted beauty, the tender rose. She is what the Bible calls his glory. She is Eve. She is created a woman!

I slept but my heart was awake. Listen! My lover is knocking: "Open to me, my sister, my darling, my dove, my flawless one. My head is drenched with dew, my hair with the dampness of the night." I have taken off my robe—must I put it on again? I have washed my feet—must I soil them again? My lover thrust his hand through the latch-opening; my heart began to pound for him. I arose to open for my lover, and my hands dripped with myrrh, my fingers with flowing myrrh, on the handles of the lock.

Song of Songs 5:2–5 (NIV)

You were created to be what you would have been if life hadn't hardened you. Don't allow the enemy to rob you of your essence and steal the fragrance from your rose. I know you were tired of being hurt, but isn't it also true that you are tired of hiding? Aren't you tired of hiding the creative things that you would like to do? Aren't you tired of suppressing any sign of concern beneath that corporate, dressed-for-success coat of armor you wear? Part of your healing requires that you come out of hiding and stand in the light. Stand with God, who made you like you are for a reason. You will never fulfill your destiny dressed in someone else's clothes. We need you. Your absence creates a vacancy that we must have filled.

Women's liberation is not a movement. It is a mentality. It should be the mentality that frees the woman, not only from oppression, but also from the fear of exploring her own sensitivity and uniqueness. Liberation begins when you are free to be yourself and recognize that the strength of a woman is different but no lesser than the strength of a man. The woman has strength in silk wrappings, but it is strength nonetheless.

In her youth, she was covered with frills and bows. In her adulthood, she was silhouetted in class. In her maturity, she was demure and sedately assured. Have you seen her? Can you remember her? Or has she vanished in the night, unnoticed and unobserved? Has anyone noticed that we are losing a generation of women who have transformed before our eyes into some mutated synthetic replacement for what once was? It reminds me of the storyline of some midnight horror movie. The bodies are still there, but the insides have been pulled out. They have been pulled like an engine is pulled from the sleek body of a shiny new car. It is as if an alien spaceship is yanking the very essence of our women away. Perhaps it is not the coming of the alien that has robbed us of our mothers, our daughters, and our wives. Perhaps it is the result of too much pain, too many questions, and too few answers that has left us with rollers in the drawer, stockings in the sink, but no soft-skinned, soft-scented lady left to hold in the night.

Hasn't anyone noticed that the gleam is dying in her eyes? Does no one care that the tinkle has gone from her laughter! Is this not a crime to watch the destruction of her living, vibrant heart? She is the soul of the house. She is the heart of the marriage. She is the hope of the children and the life support of her lover, her husband, her man!

> She maketh fine linen, and selleth it; and delivereth girdles unto the merchant. Strength and honour are her clothing; and she shall rejoice in time to come. She openeth her mouth with wisdom; and in her tongue is the law of kindness. She looketh well to the ways of her household, and eateth not the bread of idleness. Her children arise up, and call her blessed; her husband also, and he praiseth her.
>
> Prov. 31:24–28

This woman is the Mother Teresa of ministry. She is the Eleanor Roosevelt of politics. She is the Coretta Scott King of civil rights. She has been abducted by this society. She has been ransomed for more money, equal rights, and a corner office. She is entitled to all of that and more, but the fight to attain it has depleted her and denied us of her beauty. We must win her back. But we cannot if no one notices she is missing.

I tell you now that you are going to see the emergence of women who are celebrating their femininity. They will have success and the respect of executives and still enjoy motherhood and family. The woman's world has widened. Women can go further and achieve more and still be feminine. But more important, Christian women will find themselves inspired by their faith and fueled by their convictions. They will be able to have the balance that was once denied them. You will see men rising up and blessing women, saying, "She is my star." The enemy has tried for years to wage a war between the sexes. He has tried in our boardrooms, our bedrooms, and even our pulpits. We must realize that we were designed to work together. Our strength is in the variance of our strategies. The mistake of the past is man's oppression of woman, but the mistake of the future is this spirit whereby the woman imitates the masculine strength and we lose the creative edge of her feminine perspectives!

Perhaps the challenges of our times have laid to rest all hopes of reviving the gentle femininity that once sat on porches and sipped tea in the gentle breezes of softer times. But beneath the straight-lined suits and hard-as-nails exterior, can you hear the cries within the hearts of many women who wish life would afford them, once again, the luxury of being pampered by gentlemen who think them far too exquisite to be exposed to rowdy conversations and boisterous communications? Is the lady not a casualty of war? Is she not the victim of the emasculation of men and the chaos of the times? Is she the sad result of a life filled with too much work and no play? She is the fatality that evolves from too many empty promises. She is on a love-deficient diet that has turned into anorexia of the soul. A life of distraught times and adverse conditions has taken away from us the lady whom we all needed. She is replaced by hard lines and tough will. But late in the night, we all mourn her loss. Even she mourns the passing of the hope and optimism that once enveloped her like a warm blanket on a cold winter's night. It would not be so terrible if men alone missed her. But I have seen the quick glances in the mirror and the long looks through the window, and I know what few men realize. She herself is mourning the loss of the woman that she wanted to be. She is mourning the loss of the woman she started to be. She is strong. She is a survivor, but still . . . still somehow beneath the weathered exterior, she is mourning.

She Shall Be Called Woman

This may sound like folly to the girl who survived the street by her wits. She cannot indulge herself in the time-consuming reverie of lost loves and hidden needs. She has trained herself to endure. She has taught herself not to ask and not to need, and whenever possible, not to cry. It must sound like fodder to the woman who reared her children alone, working two jobs, bathing her soft skin with the callused hands of hard work. It sounds too expensive to consider, too lofty to contemplate, in the mind of someone whose life has been abusive and to whom society has been indifferent. But allow us this moment for you and me to fantasize.

May I hold your hand while we stroll down a long winding trail into the intrinsic need of the human heart? Let's just continue walking far beyond the cold pavement of our indifferent society, back into the flowered garden of the Creator's masterful plan. Let's follow the winding trail of a truth etched on the thin porous pages of Holy Scriptures. It is sad that we have produced a generation of seekers who look everywhere for answers rather than consider the owner's manual, the blueprint to life, the encyclopedia for survival, and the compass for direction—the Word of God.

The Word of God has never been fully appreciated for its medicinal purpose in treating the sick souls of a depraved humanity. That describes all of us who, in varying forms and to diverse degrees, have been mutilated by life's dark tragedies. It is the great emancipator of the enslaved and the demeaned. To the woman it is no less liberating. Its truth, though interlaced with roles and restrictions, is ultimately intended to assist in weaving the woman into the greatest liberty she has ever known. The Bible is written to ensure the feminine heart the boundaries and the restrictions needed to protect her from exploitation. Yes, it teaches submission. It teaches it without apology. But the connoisseur of life will tell you that all of us submit to something and often to someone. But the Bible warns her to submit through marriage to one man, and not because of his gender, but because of his position of covering and protection. He is there for her covering. He is the fur she curls up in and feels warmed. He is the man whom she incidentally selects by her acceptance of his invitation. She should accept the invitation only when she feels she has found the one who has the capacity to love as Christ loved the church. That is to say, he is self-sacrificing and giving of himself for her. Who wouldn't submit to, honor and obey, and hum the vows all night long to this prince? You tell me, modernist, who couldn't submit to a love like that!

When Eve was created, she was heralded onto the face of the planet like a bride who is carried across the threshold of a new home. She was not created until all of her needs were provided. She was the climax of the creation. She was the grand finale. She is unlike her male counterpart, who was created with everything except a companion. She was reserved and held until all things were in place and the stage had been set. She steps onto the stage only when every prop had been carefully contemplated by a God who cares enough to give the very best and is rhythmic enough to know the timing that is required to bring her forward in step with all that he had created.

Her backdrop was the earth. The only thing that covered her soft, satiny skin was the bright yellow rays of the sun. In the night, the moonlight cradled her breast with tender hands and a radiant glow. She may have showered in the cascading current of a rapid waterfall. As she ran, her strong thighs whipped through the tall grain with a synergy that cannot be adequately described. Though she was created last, she was in no way an afterthought. She was planned and crafted to the slightest detail. He designed her cycles and systems. He designed her breasts and their function. Even her escort was designed compatible and attracted. There was no struggle to bond. She was the apple of his eye. She was the energy in his stride and the strength in his body. She possessed his same composition, and in his arms, love found its definition. She was not left parading around alone.

Her escort was the first and only created son of God. Eve was the first womb he had known. He was not birthed through a womb, nor born in selfish sin, nor shaped in iniquity. He was hollowed out of the hand of God Himself. His name was Adam—prince of the palace of life. His strong, glistening flesh, bulging biceps, and broad chest made him stand apart from all other life in the garden. His long, tailored legs, straight posture, and commanding presence showed the superior quality that comes from being tutored by God and mentored in His presence alone. He walked through the garden as though he was the chief commanding officer, and in fact he really was. Their playground was the mountains, and their bedroom stood by the roaring rivers of the Euphrates.

Were they in love? you ask. Of course! She was created especially for him, to meet his every need and want. The one that formed her did it with him in mind. And God taught Adam how to love her. He brought his two children together and made them a family. Both of their interests were met in one act! One act so staggering that the angels were awed and the stars glistened as if their eyes were wet with tears. This was the wedding of the universe. The fruit of their love has populated the planet, created the automobile, examined the atom, forged into science, soared through the air, and explored the galaxy. It is the fusion of two entities with the climactic thunder of the Master's approval.

When it was finished he said what all lovers say when love is right and the night is well. He said, "And it was good and very good." One statement released them and the two were forever one. Love is far better with His approval than it would ever be without it. After all, he has designed it for our good and His glory.

Now, the man he chose for her was not weak. He might have been meek, but he was certainly not weak, and he was not broken. It never works when a woman marries a man thinking that her presence is required to mend him. If he is broken when she meets him, he will not be fixed when she marries him. When Adam was introduced to Eve, he was a man on his way. She was to add to him, accessorize him. She was to be a "help meet" to him. But you cannot help someone who isn't on his way!

> And the LORD God said, It is not good that the man should be alone; I will make him a help meet for him.
> Gen. 2:18

Adam was in authority when she saw him. He had her quarters prepared, and her garden was plush with weeping willows and tender lilies. The roses released their fragrance and the soft scent of the honeysuckle filled the air when He presented the first bride to the first groom, and the heavens clapped their hands. She was there, the one, the star in flesh, the soft center of a budded rose. The first human taste of sensual, sensitive, feminine flesh and Adam could only exclaim, "Whoa man!" And that she was. She was a woman. Fashioned out of the same clay, she was strangely similar to the man, but completely different. Her uniqueness intrigued him; her similarity gave him comfort. He could not lie with beast or fowl; they were too foreign to his composition. But this girl smelled like fresh meat to a hungry heart. She was a woman. She was his lady.

Soon she was called to more than love and romance. She was called to assist God in creation. She was called to be a mother. She was called to another kind of love—the maternal love to which most women eventually gravitate.

Perhaps one of the most difficult challenges any woman faces is the task of balancing her role as a lover with her call to be a mother. In a moment, so much is changed. From a wife to a mother, from a couple to a family. Yesterday, Eve was

Adam's lover, his playmate, his lady. Today she's changing diapers and nursing sons. Time that was once Adam's alone is now shared with her duties as a mother. Although a child brings great joy to a home, he also brings great change. A woman is sometimes torn between her role as a wife and her job as a mother. This is something a man might not understand. All he knows is that his lady is not there when he rolls over in the night. She is either too tired or rocking the cradle. Sometimes he feels alone, and his loneliness becomes a source of contention. Many times he foolishly miscommunicates his love for her with words that sound more like frustration. If only someone could express to her what he really means: "Honey, I miss you. I feel alone without you. I love the mother in you, but I still need the lover in you." We know that we need to talk, but what we do not know is that men and women speak in different tongues. Most marriages are destroyed because we do not speak the same language. I have spent more time interpreting for couples than counseling them. Most do not know each other's language even after years of marriage.

The challenge to the man is to communicate to his lady what he may feel embarrassed to admit. This is difficult. How can he tell her that he's jealous of his own child? He's not necessarily jealous, but that is what it will sound like, won't it? How can he tell her that he's tired of her being tired, without sounding selfish? So he does what most men do with difficult issues: he buries them in silence. And day by day, glitter falls from his twinkling eyes, and silence is printed on his lips. The lovers become partners and the tension grows.

The first question a man will face is Can a mother still be my lady? It is not the only question. There will be more. There will be questions such as Can the busy working woman still be my lady? Can the PTA board member, carpooling, soccer mom still be my lady? These are the questions that men lack the courage to ask. When they do ask them, it is often in an argumentative way. A man may even become intimidated by his wife's interest in the church. He does not resent her spiritual involvement, he just misses her. He doesn't know how to tell her that he is tired of hearing her rant about how wonderful the pastor is or how she wishes he were more considerate, like the pastor. So instead he complains and does just the opposite of her request. He becomes sullen or angry, and gradually he becomes someone so different from the man she married that she wonders the same question that God asked: "Adam, where art thou?"

> By night on my bed I sought him whom my soul loveth: I sought him, but I found him not. I will rise now, and go about the city in the streets, and in the broad ways I will seek him whom my soul loveth: I sought him, but I found him not. The watchmen that go about the city found me: to whom I said, Saw ye him whom my soul loveth?
>
> Song of Songs 3:1–3

When Adam is missing, the lady is lost. He was the tune for which she was created; she is the harmony that surrounds his melody. But if his melody stops, her harmony fades and the concert ends in silence. Who knows exactly what happens? She asks herself every night as he sleeps, "Adam, where art thou?" He wakes in the morning and glances at her and asks, "Who can find the virtuous woman?" They have lost each other, and the music that used to fill the garden becomes noise in the streets!

He often disappears into his work, his ministry, or his mistress. She just drifts into other pursuits. She is after all a "help meet." She was designed to achieve a vision, if not his, somebody else's, if not somebody else's, why not her own? And so around and around she goes and where it stops no one knows. Finally when we see her again, she is alone—alone with two teenage children, a three-bedroom apartment, an empty bed, and a closet full of clothes. The lady has come a long way from dancing naked in the evening wind of the courts of Eden. She has leaped from the kitchen to the courtroom, from the bedroom to the boardroom. Her life has been transformed. Looking back, she smiles, for through it all God has been good. It is her time now. It is the hour of her emergence. Still, something is missing. She's like a bare wall in a beautiful museum; we wonder what would have been there, what should have been there. She says it doesn't matter—but does it?

Chapter Five

A Woman with Balance

For the Christian woman, there is a pursuit for balance. She knows that the only way she can be complete is to be balanced. She will veer neither to the right nor to the left. Her gentle hands hold tight the stern that guides the ship, demanding that her course not be compromised by her ambitions or goals. She seeks to be proof positive that it is possible to have the attention of her mate and the respect of her contemporaries. Why not have it all? That is excellence. The woman of Proverbs 31 had it all. But balance is very difficult to achieve. And it's not just time that needs to be balanced; a woman has the exhausting task of balancing her many roles. She must change clothes like Houdini and move from scene to scene without confusing her roles. It is difficult to go from feeling like a workhorse all day, to a mommy all evening, to a honey pot at night. This task is accomplished only if a woman basks often in the light of God's word and seeks Him for creative ways to balance herself. It cannot be done without prayer. It cannot be done without God. Perhaps that is how he meant for life to be: completely unattainable without Him. Perhaps He knew that if we could successfully navigate it without Him, we would become so engrossed in what He gave us that we would eventually forget the one who gave it to us in the first place.

> And he is before all things, and by him all things consist. Col. 1:17

We need God to attain it, but we also need him to maintain what we have been blessed to attain. The prayer for today is simple: "Lord, help me hold it all together." Whisper it in the morning. Whisper it throughout the day. It is the spiritual supplement of champions. It is the secret source of strength for virtuous women. The power of simple God-conscious prayer is all you need. It is important that you say to Him, "Lord, I need you!" We are so busy asking for things that we sometimes forget to ask for Him. And He is the one who holds it all together.

It is intimidating to wrestle with a life that is so full that it drips over the side like a coffee cup overfilled. The saucer collects the remains of what the cup cannot hold. "Lord," she cries, "catch what I could not hold and hold it for me until tomorrow." He has a way of giving to all who seek it a grace that enables every cup to have a saucer. If your cup is overflowing, ask Him to be your saucer and catch what you are letting slip. But remember to recapture what He caught, for grace is just for a short while. If He has held it by grace, you must manage it soon. Find a strategy to manage what He has given you.

The virtuous woman must wear many hats, but none too tightly that she cannot change to the next. She is a woman who has all four seasons in her life span. Her life is in a receiving mode in the spring and filled to flooding in the summer. It slows down from stress in the fall, and in the winter of her life, she sits on the porch and wishes she had something more to do. There will be a day when all of us, men and women alike, will wish that we had the challenges that we have now to consume our thoughts. This stage may be chaotic, but it will not last long. Enjoy the madness, organize the challenges, and every so often change those hats.

Refreshed, Refueled, and Refired

You must not become such a workhorse that you cease to be a person. Learn from men. They golf, laugh, play, and diversify. It is essential to survival. The lady must be a mother and then put the children to bed, sink down into a hot tub of sudsy water, listen to soft, sultry music, release the tension, and go into another mode. Do you have another mode? Every one of us needs another mode. To be one-dimensional is boring to others and lethal to our own well-being. Make time, create ways that you can refresh your well of water before everyone drains you dry. They will do it innocently enough and then grieve when you are in the hospital because you have not taught them where your boundaries are located. God sets boundaries for the sea, so you know He sets boundaries for you as His daughter.

... [who] enclosed the sea with doors, when, bursting forth, it went out from the womb; When I made a cloud its garment, and thick darkness its swaddling band, and I placed boundaries on it, and I set a bolt and doors, and I said, "Thus far you shall come, but no farther; and here shall your proud waves stop"? Job 38:8–11 (NAS)

Everything God creates has boundaries. Even though you have many responsibilities and the Bible says that to whom much is given much is required, you still need rest and a break from dealing with the same things all the time. If you are going to maintain your creative edge, you must wear each hat but change them easily. Be careful not to bore yourself to death. If you do, you will bore those who once thought you were so exciting. Keep yourself alive by diversifying your interests. Most people who live a long time have diverse interests and are multidimensional.

You are more than the many roles you play. That is how you can play them. It is because you transcend your assignment. Do not get typecast and stuck in one dimension. The lady is all things and needs to do many things, yet she remains autonomous of things she can do. Just because you can do it doesn't mean you ought to be it. You need to separate who you are from what you can do. If you don't, you can get stuck, forever identified by the role you play. Others only see the job you perform and never recognize the person you are. Even worse is when *you* lose track of who you are. Your sense of self becomes based solely on the role you play, but when you are no longer required or able to fill that role, you become lost because you don't know who you are. It's like a star athlete who spends his entire life training for the game. He thinks to himself, Why worry about school? Why learn a trade? I'm going to be a football star. And then one day he breaks his leg and can no longer play. In an instant, everything he was ceases to exist.

The same thing happens to the woman who has children and completely immerses herself in her role as mother. Then her children grow up and leave home, and she's left sitting in an empty nest wondering what to do next. She may turn back to her husband and try to pick up where she left off before her babies were born. But her role as wife has been vacant for so long, she's forgotten

100

how to fill it, and her husband got tired of waiting for her years ago and went on ahead without her. She's left confused, depressed, and alone. She spent so much time being a mother that she forgot how to be a woman.

In a marriage, the woman must wear many hats. She's a partner, a lover, a mother, and a friend. In the space of a few hours, she can go from running a business to washing clothes to reading bedtime stories to climbing into bed for a little after-dark fun. What a challenge to do it all, but how dangerous to get stuck in one role at the expense of another! Balance is the key. And remember, all these roles are things you do, not who you are.

With all these roles to fill, a woman must be careful not to burn out. There comes a point where even the lady who has great balance has to say, "That is enough. I am tired, and I need to be replenished." Different things replenish different people. Find something that refuels and invigorates you. Whether it is a facial or reading a book in the park, steal away to do it. Remember that all withdrawals and no deposits will make any account become overdrawn. Do not become angry or disappointed because those around you continue to place more and more weight on you. It is your responsibility to say when you have had enough. No one is a mind reader. You have to indicate to them when you have had enough. If you never say to those around you, "I am taking time for me," they will not think that you need it. The only way to endure the demands placed on you is knowing when to put up your hand and say, "Enough!" It is helpful to direct those you love to an endless source rather than being that endless source. Become a compass, a guide, and avoid becoming everyone's final destination. It is wise to be a means and not an end. Serve them, love them, and then direct them to someone who never fails them. Understand that you are not the Christ, just a star. The godly woman is a star. She is a star that will shine in the night. She will direct both men and women back to the pursuit of the baby Jesus. She is the lady who dares to be distinctively different from others. She is progressive enough to be an entrepreneur, but she is also wise enough to clothe her children in humility and adorn them with the wisdom that she gleaned from her plights in life.

This is the kind of woman men will pursue. She need not be too available. She is too precious to be predictable and available to every onlooker who passes by her. Men may pursue lewd women, but they generally do not value them or marry them. Anything that is too common diminishes in value. He must feel that he has something rare and sacred. Something fragile and special is to be treasured and appreciated. Many times if a woman has been through a lot and brings a lot of history to the table, she may have trouble seeing herself as valuable. But you must make a fresh start and see yourself as special. If you do not, history will just repeat itself.

It is my prayer that your past does not harden you. I want you to be refreshed so you can resist the temptation to become a rock of indifference. Few men are attracted to something hardened and callused. A woman of excellence is not the toy that all men play with; she is the fragile glass decanter that we all behold and admire. A man knows the difference. His speech is modified in her presence. She is a table marked "reserved." She is an exhibit marked "look but do not touch." She is the envy of the ordinary and the object of the connoisseur. She is the goal of her daughter and the gem of her husband. Her words are far more glamorous than her clothes. She is rich, whether she lives in the projects or a condominium. She is covered with the jewels of glistening eyes and the luster of hope. Age cannot rob her, for she is far more than smooth skin and strong bones. She is as fine in white hair as she was in youth. Class is always timeless. She is not the faddish, foolish, fanatical icon of the day. She is as timeless as a concerto in C minor. But madam, beware of life's vampires. These are the bloodsucking situations that come into all of our lives. Do not allow them to rob you of the gleam in your eye and the hope in your heart. Beware of the wicked one and all of his tools that are against you. When God creates the woman in the Book of Genesis, the very first prophecy is one that suggests there will be war between her and Satan forever. He despises her, and the feeling is mutual. The dark, sinister force would love the opportunity to break into the treasure chest of your femininity and steal the glistening stones from your heart. He would leave you empty if he could. Do not let him. Now, understand that this enemy does not come in a red suit with a tail. Nor does he come in an obvious fashion. He is a thief. He dresses for the night. He drapes himself in secrecy and may parade himself in your life as a terrible childhood or a corrupt first marriage. He wears many outfits, but his purpose is always the same. Hide your treasure deep within. Hide it so far away that the rainy gusts of wind that come to all of us will not blow away your desire for future experiences. If that happens, you have been robbed, my lady. You have been robbed.

Many women have been robbed. They are outwardly successful but inwardly impoverished. Life has robbed them of optimism. They trust no one. They expect nothing, and they are hard to convince. These are the casualties of war. They lost their treasure to some pained incident that snatched away their hope. Even after the incident is over and there is someone new in their lives, they are so pained by the past that they have not fully been able to open their hearts again. No one can pump life through a broken heart. It is like pouring perfume into a broken decanter. No matter what you put in it, it always leaks out again. If your heart has been broken by life, if your optimism has died in the fight to endure, I challenge you; I speak resurrection to you now. The pain diminishes, and the fear will subside. Life is still worth living to all who believe. This is a time of recovery. You cannot recover in anger or denial. Come out of the dark memories and into the light.

Initially you may have to protect your heart and plant your trust and hope in God. In the middle of a stormy attack, hide it in Christ. He is the rock that the hurting can hide in. He is the refuge for the storm victims. He will not allow the burglar to vandalize you again. Hide your heart in him. He will heal you so that he can use you again. He will heal you until you are free to trust and love again. Life without passion and love is like a dry steak that has been cooked to the point that its leathery texture is void of juice and bitter to taste.

Guard your heart but do not hide your face. God is not through with you. He has a plan for you. If you lose your optimism, the enemy has won. Place your hope with the power of God. Place your future in the hands of God. Don't you know that God is too wise to leave your destiny in the hands of your enemy? Don't you know that God had something special in mind when He made you? He had a specific role that only you can play. Refuse to forfeit His plan just because of your pain. Bear it like a woman in labor. Know that the pain will pass, and the promise will be delivered. Bear it knowing that the pain cannot steal what the Lord has promised. Often, pain is the midwife that God uses to help us birth the greatness that is deep in the fibers of our souls. That pain is an alarm in the woman that announces to her that the baby is coming. If you have been in pain, maybe it is because the baby is coming. The baby is the destiny that God is birthing in your life, and the pain is a sure indication that you are getting close to your delivery. This is no time to faint now, dear lady. Grab the sides of the bed and push!

> Now why dost thou cry out aloud? is there no king in thee? is thy counsellor perished? for pangs have taken thee as a woman in travail. Be in pain, and labour to bring forth, O daughter of Zion, like a woman in travail: for now shalt thou go forth out of the city, and thou shalt dwell in the field, and thou shalt go even to Babylon; there shalt thou be deliver of thine enemies.
>
> Mic. 4:9–10

It is your seed that will bruise the head of your enemy, not you. That is why you cannot stop until you deliver everything that God has implanted within you. I say to you, lady, Arise! There is a king within your womb, and he is kicking with life in your spirit. It is the child of destiny, the seed of tomorrow, and the wind of expectation. Do not abort it. Nurture it, squeeze it, feed it, but do not lose it. It is the King. It is the Christ in you. The hope and the glory. In fact, you will realize that all that you need to survive is already somewhere in the womb waiting to be birthed. In short, you are pregnant with your own deliverance. The next push might be the one that delivers you of all your past.

The search is on for the woman who can deliver up to her generation a virtue that is distinct. She is the merging of Eve and Sarah. All of her generation will be blessed through her survival. In each generation and every culture there are a few women who are so endowed that even critics clap and shed tears in memory of them. These are the mothers of the masses. We do not always get to know them, but we behold the effects they have on the world. Their excellence comes through camera lenses, is seen in print, and is realized in their children. These are the ladies-in-waiting who make up the Queen's court! These ladies are the Jackie Os and Coretta Scotts, whose soft strength and stately demeanor transcend our differences and quiet our criticisms. We have caught glimpses of truly fascinating women who have the wise eyes of a Mother Teresa and the gentle touch that warms our soul like hot milk served by a grandmother on a sleepless night. These women, who hail from varying backgrounds and suggest differing opinions and moral perceptions, possess an element of class that transcends diversity. They show us how to survive pain and endure grief. Their strength does not demean men; it affirms them. Theirs are the breasts that men draw hope from. They are the mothers of the mighty. They have been the mothers of creativity in the lives of some whom they will never even get to meet. We gaze in awe at their poise. They are stars in the night of their generations. And we can but nod at the truth of their words and clasp our hands in their presence.

I'm reminded of my mother, a gentle woman with the strength to build a home and the power to create a family. I can easily recall the days of my youth. The smell of biscuits, the sound of laughter, and the touch of affection were everyday occurrences. Those were the days when home was a reality and not a myth that is acted out more adeptly on television screens than in the lives of those who watch. My mother belonged to a day of grace that defied finances. She was a lady not because of the abundance of wealth she possessed, but the abundance of class she demonstrated. I can still see the plain, starched dress that she had ordered from a catalog. The thin-belted waist and the flowing skirt were draped by an apron as she sashayed through the house as if it were a castle. She seemed not to notice that the roof was leaking, the floor creaking, and the screen door was in need of repair. She still brought to the house an essence of femininity that transformed the tattered building into a place that we rushed home to. Be it ever so humble, it was still home. Home, not because of its design, but because of its occupants. It was the lady who made the house become a home. My father bought the house, but that was all that he could do. He bought it, but my mother transformed it into a home. For homes cannot be bought; they must be created. Created by the heart of someone who has the ingredients of love and family orientation, which mixed with gentleness and sensitivity create an aura that lingers in the heads of children and wafts in their minds far into their adulthood.

Simply stated, my point is that you need not come from a silvery satin background to be a lady. You need not graduate from a university to be a wise woman. Ladies cannot be defined merely by their position or status. Some are married, some single. Some are domestic, while others are professional. Perhaps it is their own self-perception more than any other materialistic accomplishment that creates them. Perhaps it is their spirit that creates the mystique that enamors men and captures the hearts of children.

I cannot be sure. All I know is that I can hear the first traces of it in my daughter's laughter. I can feel it in the touch of her hand on my shoulder when I am tired. I can see it in her deep, dark, brilliant brown eyes. She is already in "Lady 101." Her courses have begun and her exams are before her. She is to be protected, not only from physical threats but also from emotional assaults. These assaults can be devastating and create immeasurable pain. We need to protect our girls so they can become women of excellence!

Chapter Six

The Lady:
A Private Garden

My darling bride is like a private garden, a spring that no one else can have, a fountain of my own. You are like a lovely orchard bearing precious fruit, with the rarest of perfumes; and saffron, calamus and cinnamon, and perfume from every other incense tree, as well as myrrh and aloes, and every other lovely spice. You are a garden fountain, a well of living water, refreshing as the streams from the Lebanon mountains.

Song of Songs 4:12–15 (TLB)

The lady is a fertile field. Her tender heart is softly turned soil that awaits the seed. She carries the potential of massive reproduction. Her mind is the incubator of dreams and the womb of greatness. She is irrigated when in love and dehydrated when hurt. She is enriched by those who love her and stripped by those who abuse her. Those whom she touches will dine on her harvest. She will be the end of someone's famine. She is a garden. She is the place where hunger is sated. She is the place where hungers will be quenched. She is the place where rich soil will produce fertile food and lives are richer because of her. She is a garden. She is the focal point of those who love her and the absolute envy of those who don't.

Yes, the lady is a garden of love and a field of potential, and it is a field that is to be carefully planted. She is as vulnerable as freshly turned soil. She is a field open and exposed. To the lady I warn, "Be careful what you grow in your garden." Or better still, be careful whom you let sow in your field. There are some things that you will not want to be seeded into your heart and your life. The Bible teaches us that words are like seeds. Whenever they are spoken, they bring forth fruit. It suggests that we as Christians are begotten by the word. That is to say that our salvation is a result of the words that are sown into us. That is why preaching is so powerful. It is word; it is seed sown. Most major changes in our country have happened as a result of words that are spoken. If the entire nation is altered by words, then you can be certain that individuals are altered by the power of words.

A childhood nursery rhyme asks this question: "Mary, Mary, quite contrary, how does your garden grow?" The question is a strong one that all Marys must answer. How does my garden grow? From whence cometh these things that have grown into my personality that corrupt the integrity of my intended purpose? Have you ever looked at yourself and thought, How in the world did I get in this situation? Have you ever seen a part of your personality get choked by the weeds of bad experiences? Mary, Mary, are you quite contrary? What made you feel that way?

> So the servants of the owner came and said to him, "Sir, did you not sow good seed in your field? How then does it have tares?" He said to them, "An enemy has done this. . . ."
> Matt. 13:27–28 (NKJ)

Many times contrary feelings are born out of seeds that are sown by adverse situations. They are often sown by people and influences that do not even stay around for the harvest. You find yourself harvesting things that you did not even plant. Every affair, relationship, and involvement that you have experienced as a woman leaves something behind. There are seeds planted by each event that are not easily uprooted. You are a garden, but only time will tell what harvest you will yield. If you have not liked what you are growing so far, look at what was sown. Whatsoever a man soweth, that shall he also reap. How does your garden grow indeed? It grows from the seeds that have been sown in your life. If you want to change what is growing, all you need do is change what is being sown or at least who is sowing it!

Guard with all diligence your soil from corrupt seeds. Many women are still suffering from misplaced, thoughtless words. It is dangerous to allow people to pour their pain into your field. It will grow in you long after they are gone. The seeds that you see growing in the field of your life have been planted either by circumstances or by persons who have spoken things in your life. I caution you with flashing lights and neon signs to guard your garden with all of your strength. Be careful whom you allow to speak into your life. It is dangerous to receive counsel from the wrong people. You need to avoid people who plant seeds that are negative and demeaning. The seeds are worse than the incidents. Seeds last a long time and bring forth fruit for years to come.

> For there are six things the Lord hates—no, seven: haughtiness, lying, murdering, plotting evil, eagerness to do wrong, a false witness, sowing discord among brothers.
>
> Prov. 6:16 (TLB)

The seventh thing is added, not as an addendum but as a climax to all that God despises. He has total disgust for those who sow seeds of discord. A seed of discord can be as minute as a suggestion or implication, yet once planted it takes root and festers like an infection, growing into an ugly weed that chokes all the flowers in your garden. Those words are the seeds that bring forth bitter roots and poison your garden. Yes, there are things it is better that you do not hear.

Look at your life and clear out the weeds

that were planted by the words of others. Replace them with the word of God, for God's word planted within the fertile ground of an open heart aborts the seeds of negativity that are inherent in you. There are some things you should be ready to abort. Words of fear and doubt will bring forth low self-esteem and intimidation. Abort them quickly. Words of hate and anger yield the fruits of bitterness and distrust. Remove those seeds before they germinate and take root.

If only people understood that abuse is not always physical or sexual. One of the hardest abuses to be healed from is verbal abuse. It receives little sympathy, but it is as deadly and dangerous as any known to man. Sadly, many who attack with words do it because it is the crime least likely to be prosecuted and is seldom detected or reported. To some it is a game of wit. It is a chance for those who specialize in wicked words to display their craft and smugly laugh at the effect. Tragically, they do not realize that their tongues are quick enough to win the debate and lethal enough to destroy the opponent. If you have been a victim, rush to the word of God and abort the words of hate. If you have been the perpetrator, find another way to relieve frustration. Your words are deadly, far more lethal than a gun. They will bruise the soul and scar the spirit.

I sense that even now there are some of you who can still hear the piercing words that cut through every success and mock every conquest. Like ghosts, these words haunt you. Somewhere in your life, someone said hurtful things that got lodged in your spirit. I tell you again, turn to the word of God. Only He can excavate the seeds that bring forth the fruit of your unhappiness. You need to be able to move on to greater things in your life. You need to be the garden that nurtures the world and feeds your own soul. Sow the word of God and you will reap the rewards of a lifetime.

Who can find a virtuous woman? for her price is far above rubies. The heart of her husband doth safely trust in her, so that he shall have no need of spoil. She will do him good and not evil all the days of her life. She seeketh wool, and flax, and worketh willingly with her hands. She is like the merchants' ships; she bringeth her food from afar. She riseth also while it is yet night, and giveth meat to her household, and a portion to her maidens. She considereth a field, and buyeth it: with the fruit of her hands she planteth a vineyard. She girdeth her loins with strength, and strengtheneth her arms. She perceiveth that her merchandise is good: her candle goeth not out by night. She layeth her hands to the spindle, and her hands hold the distaff. She stretcheth out her hand to the poor; yea, she reacheth forth her hands to the needy. She is not afraid of the snow for her household: for all her household are clothed with scarlet. She maketh herself coverings of tapestry; her clothing is silk and purple. Her husband is known in the gates, when he sitteth among the elders of the land. She maketh fine linen, and selleth it; and delivereth girdles unto the merchant. Strength and honour are her clothing; and she shall rejoice in time to come. She openeth her mouth with wisdom; and in her tongue is the law of kindness. She looketh well to the ways of her household, and eateth not the bread of idleness. Her children arise up, and call her blessed; her husband also, and he praiseth her. Many daughters have done virtuously, but thou excellest them all. Favour is deceitful, and beauty is vain: but a woman that feareth the Lord, she shall be praised. Give her of the fruit of her hands; and let her own works praise her in the gates.   Prov. 31:10–31

A truly good woman is a wife before she is married. Neither bridal showers nor books can produce in her what has not been inbred. There is within her the unique gift of nurturing that makes her exemplary. She is a carefully calculated mix of strength and vulnerability. Refined and fragile, strong and stable. She is a giving woman whose life's goal reaches far beyond her own need for fulfillment and anchors in the warm feeling that erupts from touching others.

To produce a radiant wedding ring, you must start with a high-grade gem that is precut and brilliant. One cannot take just any stone and make it into a wedding ring. The criteria are quite specific. The jewel must be of exquisite quality if the ring is going to twinkle through life with luster and vitality. Likewise, the criteria for being a wife are very specific. She cares for the needs of others and has the ability to find fulfillment through giving and sharing herself with others. There is far more required to be a wife than merely being a woman. Every woman is not a wife. Hence, the Scripture declares, "Whoso findeth a wife findeth a good thing." That Scripture would be ridiculous if the issue were only about finding a woman. No one needs to look far to find a woman. It is the pursuit of a wife that is a challenge, as challenging as digging through a mountain of stones to find a diamond. And like a high-quality gem, these characteristics have to be inherent to the woman. They can't be bought or learned. They can't be forced or formulated. A good wife is a diamond, a treasure that must be mined. Anything else is just a rhinestone. Sure, it may glitter for a while, but it won't be long before it shatters like the piece of glass it really is.

Many foolish men have plunged headlong into the ditch of despair trying to create a jewel from a common rock. It is the wise young man who, like a miner, knows that he can only hope to discover what God has already created. She is to be sought after, and when she is found she will always be appreciated. He must know that those things that come easily generally tarnish quickly. Lord, help us to find the treasure that You have already created in women.

Somewhere there is an excellent wife waiting to be discovered. It is she whom You would use to bless the life of some excellent man whose help is in her. She is the missing ingredient that will complete his vision. She is a woman of many resources. Her soil is rich, though her land may be barren. When he plants his greatness in her fertile ground, she will flourish. She is a rich composite of many precious potentials. Many of them she may have realized without him, but when they unite each should enhance the other. Look deeply, O suitor, who stalks the night waiting on the one that will make his life complete. She has hidden treasure deep within her. It may be buried treasure. It may be buried beneath pain and secrets, scars and fears, but it is a treasure nonetheless. It is often hidden beneath a rough exterior that acts as a camouflage and occasionally discourages men who would normally dig feverishly to find her. The search is on and the need is great for the woman of excellence. To find her would mean the man has hit the lottery of life! To keep her and cherish her would enrich his existence to the height of living. Her presence alone should cause him to feel a sense of wealth so opulent that he accrues great gain and interest.

She is in a moment a treasure to be admired. In a lifetime she is an investment paying dividends to all to whom she is exposed. She is a lady of majesty and elegance. Her riches are beyond counting. She is adorned with diamonds in her eyes and rubies in her smile. She is the jasper stone of the day and the rich onyx of the night.

Her worth cannot be known in a moment, but it will show in a crisis. It is then that a man will know she is authentic and not fraudulent. It is then that life portrays so well the difference between rhinestones and diamonds. It is in the crises of life that a lady herself begins to realize the magnitude of her own creativity. During each crisis, she is appraised and her value only grows. With every test and trial, she appreciates and is appreciated. But the greatest appreciation that causes her to be whole must come from within her before it comes from around her. She must know that she is a woman of excellence. Not a woman of arrogance, but a woman of excellence. This is the spirit of a virtuous woman.

It is dangerous for all to know your worth and you not know it yourself. If you do not know what you have, you will not know when you lose it. It is only when one is aware of a treasure that it is treated with respect and kept away from villains and opportunists. Do you know your own worth, O woman of virtue? Your knowing it is not boasting. It is affirming yourself so that you will have the virtue to affirm others. It is almost impossible to give out to others what has not been deposited.

You are rich. You are loaded with wonder and filled with splendor. You are created in Christ Jesus and swaddled in his radiance. Your potentials are limited only by your own vision. Aspire to the heavens and reach out for the wind. What God has implanted will show through your life in the end. Hurl yourself at the challenge. You are the galling wind of a hurricane and yet the tender swaying of a branch. You are as hard as a diamond and as soft as the black velvet that enhances the brilliance of the jewel. You are a woman of virtue. Shine, lady, shine!

The Lady Has an Enemy

Woman is a precious commodity. Through her all greatness is born. She is the mother of nations, the womb of creativity, the garden of life. But it is precisely her great value that makes her the target of evil. The lady has an enemy, and it is Satan himself. He is the one who knows that when men and women come together they give birth, and it is his goal to keep them apart. His strategy against women has always been deception. He employed this tactic with Eve in the Garden of Eden and he has not changed his method. Eve would never have knowingly brought evil to Adam. She thought she was doing something good and positive. She was misled by the master deceiver. He led her down the path of sin.

> And [it was] not Adam [who] was deceived, but the woman being quite deceived, fell into transgression.
> I Tim. 2:14 (NAS)

I want to talk about the method of Satan's deception. The Scripture declares that there would be a conflict between the seed of the woman and the seed of the serpent. There would be conflict between the woman and the enemy. Anyone who understands warfare realizes that it is necessary to study the tactics of your enemy, so you might be more successful in defeating him. You know his methods, so you will be prepared for his attack and ready with a strong defense. Knowledge is power; the more you know, the more powerful you become. So let us strategize and try to understand the tactics of our spiritual opponent, let us prepare as a soldier who is getting ready to face his enemy.

1. He appealed to her need to communicate.

> Now the serpent was more subtle than any beast of the field which the LORD God had made. And he said unto the woman, Yea, hath God said, Ye shall not eat of every tree of the garden? And the woman said unto the serpent, We may eat of the fruit of the trees of the garden: But of the fruit of the tree which is in the midst of the garden, God hath said, Ye shall not eat of it, neither shall ye touch it, lest ye die. And the serpent said unto the woman, Ye shall not surely die: For God doth know that in the day ye eat thereof, then your eyes shall be opened, and ye shall be as gods, knowing good and evil.
>
> Gen. 3:1–5

He engaged in a conversation with her and enticed her with speech. Lies cloaked in smooth words beguiled her. It is still his tactic today. Words are some of the strongest weapons against women. Women are, by nature, communicators. They treasure conversation. They use it to articulate their needs and appreciate it as a means to understand others. They value words so much that, used correctly, they can win a woman's heart.

Any womanizer will tell you that his hook is in his conversation. He lures women through speech. Any pastor will tell you that the most difficult thing to get women to do in a ministry is be silent. Any husband will tell you that whenever there is anything going on in the family the first thing a woman wants to do is discuss it. Satan took advantage of this love of communication to deceive Eve. He still employs this method today. He is the womanizer trapping a woman in an abusive relationship. He is a false friend leading a woman down the road to temptation. He is the manipulator, using harsh words and cruel criticism to make a woman feel worthless. Words are a powerful tool for evil. Women, beware!

But a woman's innate love for communication can also be her ally. She is the most formidable prayer warrior the church has ever seen. Her ability to articulate and her need to discuss make her a powerful force that is unstoppable in bombarding heaven. She gets release through communicating, and she is a weapon against Satan whenever she uses her propensity to speak for the purpose it was created. She is an arsenal of prayer and a missile of faith. She is powerful when her gift is aimed at the real target, the real enemy. The enemy is not men in general. The enemy is the spirit that may have operated in a man or woman in your past. The enemy is at work when anyone uses words to deceive you, mislead you, or cause you pain. Beware of sweet words and false promises. Beware of the fork-tongued devil whispering lies. Beware of the enemy! Pray!

2. He appealed to her need to contribute.

> . . . she took of the fruit thereof, and did eat, and gave also unto her husband with her; and he did eat.
>
> Gen. 3:6

When Eve gave the apple to Adam, she didn't intend to harm him. She was just following her instinct, her natural tendency to give and share. The maternal instincts of the woman often lead her to the role of "giver." She gives love to her companion, life to her child, warm milk to her young, and so on. Still, it is important that every woman, regardless of how independent and competent she may be, allow the man in her life to provide for the overall well-being of the family unit. Whenever the woman assumes responsibility for providing for the man, she reverses the divine order and the family unit goes into chaos.

Eve failed to realize that it is not her responsibility to give to Adam; it is his responsibility to give to her. A husband should be to the marriage what Christ is to the church—a provider. The Scripture says it is a man's duty to provide. Not doing so is contrary to God's word:

> But if any provide not for his own, and specially for those of his own house, he hath denied the faith, and is worse than an infidel.   I Tim. 5:8

Eve reversed the roles by assuming the position of provider for the marriage. Misplaced contribution tears down family order. It is not good for the man to eat out of the woman's hand. Anytime the woman is the primary breadwinner it destroys the man's self-esteem. It doesn't matter who makes the most money as much as it matters that he assumes the chief responsibility for provision. When a man is not permitted to provide for his family, he is likely to become confused, guilty, frustrated, and angry. The marriage is bound to suffer.

Now, I'm not saying that a woman shouldn't work and earn money. In fact, you may make more money than your husband. But take that money and save it, spend it, use it to buy stocks or fancy vacations. Just don't let your husband feel as if he has not provided for his own. It kills a man's spirit when he cannot take care of his family. He feels worthless, unmotivated, and defeated. If you don't let him provide for you, why should he even try? Why shouldn't he sit back and do nothing? One of the worst things a man can be is lazy. It not only hurts others, it destroys him! Please let him take care of you. Let him take care of the problems. Teach your son to take care of his family. It will not only bless them, it will help him to be whole and complete.

Don't get me wrong, women should

contribute. Woman was created to contribute. The Bible says that she is to be a "help meet" to the man. This means that she is to stand alongside him to assist him. A woman contributes to life. The man makes the deposit into her womb, and she is pregnant. She gives an egg, she gives calcium, minerals, oxygen, blood, protein, food, strength, flesh, and everything else needed for nine months of carrying a baby. Then she births it, so that she can give milk, love, and care to the child, and a mother continues to give to the child for the rest of her days.

Women have the unique ability of taking a vision and making it happen. They say behind every great man is a woman, and this is true. It takes a woman to help a man meet his goals. She can step into a company, a ministry, or a family and help meet the objectives. Women have almost single-handedly maintained the church through their giving, their generosity, and their compassion. They give of their time as well as their resources. They are natural-born contributors. Women are valuable, an indispensable part of God's plan. Ladies, continue to give what is so needed, but allow the man to fulfill his role too.

3. He appealed to her lust.

> And when the woman saw that the tree was good for food, and that it was pleasant to the eyes, and a tree to be desired to make one wise, she took of the fruit thereof, and did eat, and gave also unto her husband with her; and he did eat. Gen. 3:6

Two of the strongest weapons the enemy can use against us are lust of the flesh and lust of the eyes. Satan used both of them on Eve. She saw "that the tree was good for food." That is the lust of the flesh. He appealed to her hunger. Hunger is a legitimate need; it is a God-given need. But he deceived her into satisfying a legitimate need in a forbidden way. Eve could have satisfied her hunger with any fruit in the garden, but the serpent lured her to taste the fruit of the tree of knowledge of good and evil.

Are you wrestling with a legitimate need? Is the enemy enticing you to pursue forbidden pleasures? We must remember that when we try to satisfy ourselves in a way that is forbidden by God, in the end we only do ourselves harm. For instance, we all have the need for intimacy and affection, but if we allow that need to lead us into promiscuity, we run the risk of damaging ourselves physically and emotionally. The immediate gratification might be there, but it is destructive in the long run. Don't allow the wicked one to lure you down the path of sin; he will surely try. Protect yourself by finding shelter in the word of God.

The Bible also says that the woman saw the tree was pleasant to the eyes. That is the lust of the eyes. But you must remember that everything that looks good isn't necessarily good for you. Do not choose your companions by what they look like or the positions they hold. As the old adage goes, all that glitters is not gold. Many women are deceived by a handsome face, fancy clothes, and an expensive sports car. Evil is often wrapped in a pretty package, and the devil can shop at Armani and drive a Ferrari. It is dangerous to let externals be your guide. All the enemy has to do is show you a pretty picture, and you are hooked.

This attention to the external can be a positive trait. Women remember and record thought differently than men. Your eyes catch details that often escape the eyes of men. Use your remarkable power of observation, but don't let it rule you. My family has often escaped adversity because my wife noticed a detail that I would have overlooked. She notices people; she pays attention to their responses, attitudes, and personality traits, in a way that I might not. Her ability to observe details has allowed her to notice the symptoms of illness in our children early enough so we can treat them and take them to a doctor before they get too sick. She looks with the eyes of a mother, and our family has been blessed by her perception.

A woman's awareness of the external world can be a great benefit. Let your eyes help you see, but don't let externals blind you.

4. He appealed to her pride.

> For all that is in the world, the lust of
> the flesh, and the lust of the eyes, and
> the pride of life, is not of the Father,
> but is of the world.   I John 2:16

The pride of life is yet another great tool of evil. Pride of life is the need to be on top, the need to be ahead of others. The serpent told Eve that she would be wiser than God if she ate of fruit from the tree of life.

Wiser, stronger, better—deep down inside, we all want to be superior to others. Sometimes it's not even about being better, it's about people thinking we're better. It's about perception. We want acknowledgment. We may hide our desire for acknowledgment under the guise of wanting to be appreciated, but there is a difference. Being appreciated is about gratitude and worth. Acknowledgment is a standing ovation, a pat on the back, strokes to the ego. Wanting acknowledgment isn't bad in and of itself. But when it guides your actions, when it becomes a substitute for acting from the heart, you can make some very wrong decisions. If all you're after is acclaim, then anyone can shower you with flattery, lure you with hollow words of praise.

Yet pride isn't all bad. Taking pride in your work and your appearance is a good thing. No one would hire someone who takes no pride in her work. But pride should be self-generated. Wanting to do your best and congratulating yourself for a job well done are commendable. Ambition is the force that drives people to achieve. Women have worked hard and have come a long way. There was a time when girls weren't even taught to read. Today women graduate from the top universities, hold executive positions, help our country run, and help the world prosper. Wanting to improve yourself and do a good job are virtuous endeavors. Keep up the good work, but be careful that your pride doesn't make you fall.

The point I've been trying to make is that the enemy preys on what is good in women and perverts them for evil. Woman is a natural treasure. She is the help meet, the mother, the jewel in the crown of God's creation. Celebrate your virtues and fulfill your potential, but guard yourself carefully. Be careful whom you allow to touch your life, for you are holy and a treasure beyond compare.

Part Two

Her LOVER

Chapter Seven

Embracing
Someone Else

Two young people walk slowly down the beach holding hands. It is obvious they are in love. No, they are not groping each other or acting in any other inappropriate manner. They simply radiate peace and serenity. Their eyes reflect inner harmony. When they smile at each other, it is a look of trust, compassion, and mutual admiration. It is a very special relationship, one that is difficult to find but well worth the search. It is far easier to find the intense, burning passion that erupts like a volcano releasing the hot lava that burns through clothes, rips covers from a bed, and leaves satisfied partners panting in sweet tranquillity. Although that type of passion can be quite exhilarating, it does not necessarily indicate love. In fact, in some cases it actually hampers our ability to recognize true love. Passion can bind us and mislead us. It can distract our senses and cause us not to realize that a relationship is in trouble or, worse, dangerous to our emotional and spiritual health.

Please do not think that I am suggesting we become so sterile that we cannot just lose total control in our spouse's arms. Why would we turn something so enjoyable into a clinical exchange of bodily fluids? The marriage bed can, and should, be a place to indulge in erotic and exciting play. I just need to point out that many times we choose partners because they are physically appealing to us, and then we find that there is not enough inner attraction to sustain us as they change. And they do change. One thing about life, if you live long enough, it is the great equalizer. The young become old. The beautiful become average, and the smooth lines of youth give way to the weathered look of experience. If a relationship is based on physical attraction, what happens when physical beauty fades? What happens when the burning flames become little more than a glow? True love is stronger than that and can withstand the passage of time. In fact, true love is like a fine wine, growing sweeter as it ages.

Just the other day, a young lady pushing a man in a wheelchair came to the front of the church. His body was twisted and his face was permanently contorted into a sneer. Slumped over in his wheelchair, the man seemed oblivious to his surroundings.

I walked down the steps of our pulpit to speak with her, so that I could ascertain what their needs were. I was sure that she was an attendant assigned to care for the poor, unfortunate soul whose condition left him helpless and disfigured. I leaned down near her ear and whispered, "What may I do to assist you?" I was almost sure that she wanted prayer for her patient. I was taken aback when she introduced the man as her husband. With a strong chin and a stiff upper lip, she said that she and her husband wanted to join the church. She spoke with pride, as if he were standing beside her in a three-piece suit. I stumbled for words, embarrassed by my assumption yet sorry for their predicament. As I searched for words to answer her, she reached down to catch a stream of saliva that was extending from her husband's lips like a single strand of spaghetti. She wiped him lovingly and stood back up to continue her request. She explained that her husband had been in a terrible accident that left him almost completely incapacitated. One day he was a healthy, vibrant, virile man; the next he was as he sat before me. I had to swallow to hide my tears, as I was filled first with admiration and then with awe at this woman who could love this man and treat him with great affection. I knew that she was with a man who could no longer hold her, touch her, or whisper in her ear. I knew that he had not lovingly patted her while they dressed for church or given her a sly look of promised love and fulfillment. I knew that he had not dried her neck when she slipped out of the shower with beads of moisture kissing her skin. I knew that she had the task of taking care of him while no one took care of her.

I tell this story to underscore that life does bring changes. When we stand before a congregation, a preacher, and God, we make vows in a few minutes that we may have to keep for the next fifty years or more. We make those vows and walk into the future, an abyss of unexpected adventure that can lead to peril without warning. The vows are a blank check that destiny will write as we walk through life together. It is altogether possible that we might have to keep those vows, the ones that say for better or for worse, for richer or for poorer, in sickness and in health. Will we be able to keep those promises in the face of calamity, poverty, and infirmity?

We all want someone we can count on to stand by us through thick or thin. This is the lover who matters. Most people think being a good lover is about being able to perform sexual feats with great skill and sensitivity. That would be fine if we spent all of our lives in bed. But the truth of the matter is a good lover doesn't start or end in the bedroom. A good lover is the one who stays when all others have walked away. It does not matter if he is as agile as a cat and as sensitive as a frayed nerve ending. If he does not love you with his heart, stroking your body and teasing your senses will soon become meaningless. Loving the body is not enough. Your mind and your spirit need to be cared for too. Who cares if your man is built like an Adonis if he doesn't stand by you in a storm? His twinkling eyes mean nothing if he does not prove to be reliable in a crisis. Oh, my friend, being a good lover is more than hips, lips, and fingertips. It is the ability to hold the cold wind of life in your hot hands until the wind warms under your loving touch. It is standing by the bed until the light goes out in my eyes and you kiss my face one final time. It is the ability to stay with me until the machine stops and the ventilator ceases to pump air into my lungs, and I speak one last time or squeeze your hand. If you ever have to fight a real storm, you will need a lover, but not the kind you might normally seek. This is a lover of the day, not just the night. Lovers that deal with the day are more difficult to find than the kind that grope you in the night. If a tragedy occurs economically or, worse still, physically, will he still be your lover? I know these are sobering thoughts that people seldom consider, but they are the realities of life.

Now, I know that the word "lover" is thrown around carelessly and often misused. Since I am using it often, I must differentiate between what I am speaking of and what our times have suggested about a lover. The term is broadly applied to every conceivable type of sexual arrangement known to man. But please understand me; when I use the term "lover," I use it in the same way that the Song of Solomon uses "my beloved." I use it to describe the sanctity and holiness of a person in a committed marital relationship. But it means more than just being married. I use it to describe the partners following God's divine plan. There are married people who are not lovers. These are the adulterers, the gold diggers, the indifferent spouses. Some people have personal scars that are so deep they find it difficult to adhere to God's plan. I understand that. Being an active participant in a committed marriage is not an easy task, and many people fail at it. But just because people have a hard time living up to the role doesn't mean that the concept of holy matrimony is faulty. God's plan is perfect. It is His creatures that are not. What threatens this nation is the fact that many people have become so frustrated that they have altered the Master's plan to fit their own situation and needs. But it is illogical to redraw a map to fit the fact that we are lost. That is what we do when we enter into "pseudo" love affairs. They mimic marriage and actually mock it. I realize that many of these pseudorelationships are sincere and meaningful to the participants. But it is possible to be sincerely wrong. The word of God should be our map. We need to follow it, but if we do get lost, we should remember that throwing the map away won't help us find our way home.

Tragically, most of this generation has reduced love to sex. They are not the same things. These easy-come, easy-go affairs have no lasting substance and are much like loose garments. Loose garments are great when it's hot, but when it is cold, you need something that hugs the skin and forbids the elements to have access to you. That's what I want in a relationship, don't you? Who wants something that slips off like a bathrobe in a hailstorm? I want a relationship that will protect me from the storms of life. This should be everyone's ideal. Let's go after it. We may fall short of our goal, but woe be unto us if we lose sight of the goal altogether. Marriage is meant to be forever, and the only way for a relationship to survive the uncertainty of the future and the inevitable ups and downs of life is if true love is its foundation.

How to Make Love Last

I have observed old married couples whose wrinkled, frail hands are clasped as they stroll

148

in the park. These survivors of life attest to the authenticity of committed love. They have survived the hardships of life and endured the seasons of love. Young love is like springtime—everything is fresh and new. Green plants begin to sprout, breaking through the ground, starting to grow. The soil is rich and fertile, full of potential if it is nurtured. By summer, love is in full bloom. Vibrant flowers adorn the fields, and the sun wraps us in its warmth. By autumn, we grow comfortable. The harvest is ripe, and it's time to reap our rewards. Our children are grown and on their own. We can sit back and enjoy the fruits of our labor. When winter comes, the sky may be gray, the ground cold and hard, but true love is like an evergreen in the snowy forest. A couple who has been married for so long is still warm in the winter of love. The fire in their hearts keeps out the cold.

How do those couples do it? How do they stay together all those years? I watch them as they meander through the early-morning traffic in the park. Joggers and skaters whiz by them. Bicycles pass them on the right. But they don't seem to notice. They're aware only of each other as they walk through the park and talk. They talk and actually listen to each other. They each speak the name of their spouse with the undertones of endearment that suggest that they are as comfortable with each other as a pair of old house shoes. You know, the kind that have the imprint of your toes etched into the fabric. They're still lovers, but more than that, they're friends.

Isn't that funny? That is where we started out as little children. Two children play in the sandbox oblivious to the difference of their genitalia. They are friends—plain and simple. There are no pressures to impress. No need for virility. Can you remember the days when little boys thought that little girls were okay for friends but the idea of kissing a girl seemed silly? It was later, when we wrestled our little girl friends and suddenly felt a warm glow within, that we noticed touching her was different from touching the guys when playing a game of football. That was the first stage of love we were introduced to. It was simple and platonic. It is presexuality love. It is a love that is based more on friendship than eroticism. We lose that easy friendship when we become distracted sexually. Then we spend all of our lives trying to sex our way back into friendship. Isn't that what we finally come back to in later years as the passion ebbs

150

and the communication emerges? We end up back in the sandbox. We end up giggling on the front porch with our teeth in a glass and our wrinkled faces in a smile. We end up holding each other longer and listening to the rhythm of each other's breathing in the night. I am talking about soul mates. The relationship may be challenged, and it may even be betrayed, but when it is all over, you still have the only person you really want to talk to, the one who makes you laugh. It is the friendship that makes a marriage worth fighting for. It is not the sex. Sex lasts mere minutes, a few hours at best, but friendship is for a lifetime!

The needs of the body can be fulfilled in a few minutes at the least and a few hours if we are so inclined and endowed with the required stamina. But fulfilling the needs of the heart is an ongoing process. The aching heart screams far louder than the aching loins. What makes a lover wonderful is when he can kiss the body and reach down deeper to kiss the soul. Sex then becomes a means to something more important—spiritual commitment. Then you are not just having sex; you're making love. Sex comes easy; it's the loving that's hard to find.

Now here is the challenge required to

be sure that your relationship maintains a degree of love to go along with sex. Here is what you are going to need to build your relationship into a monument that is sustained when all is said and done. What you want to attain is the steady love experienced by siblings who know that they are spawned from the same loins and birthed from the same womb. Please do not think that I am suggesting that we retire our sexuality or diminish our passion for intimacy. I am suggesting that we balance those wonderful moments with a whole person who means something to us outside of the bedroom. I am suggesting that the root of your love has to be anchored in your admiration for the person; then add the attraction like spice to a favorite dish. The spice accentuates the dish, but it does not become the dish.

Always Marry in the Family

The reason the Bible discourages marrying nonbelievers is simple: God wants the basis of your love to be the fact that you share the same heavenly Father. Your husband should be your brother first. Your wife is also your sister. I do not mean your biological sister or brother. You are siblings of God.

It helps to choose someone who is a Christian like yourself because you have the same sovereign and basic values. Many non-Christians like to debate the Scriptures, but they do not realize that the word of God is a letter written to the people of God. A nonbeliever will likely not understand or agree with the word. The challenge to the nonbelievers is not to accept rules and regulations—first they need to embrace Christ and believe his word. Until they do that, you will be talking to them in a foreign language. It is as if you are both from different countries. They are not citizens of your country, and the laws were not written to them. As a Christian, you should choose someone who is governed by the same values as you. If you don't, you will never agree. It helps so much when couples have the same faith and philosophy of living.

Yet faith is not the only criterion you should look for in a companion. Many people of the same faith are still not related enough to make a strong marriage. So what does it take? The requirements are threefold. Your partner must satisfy your body, mind, and soul. Without a doubt, you need to have a physical attraction for your partner. Sex is one of the many pleasures of matrimony, and it should be enjoyed. Your partner should please you physically, and vice versa. What does physical pleasure matter if he does not love you as a person and as a friend? You and your partner should be of like mind, able to talk, listen, and simply enjoy each other's company. Finally, you should share similar values. You will walk together down the path in life, share the same map, and follow the same direction.

Only when all of these requirements are met will a marriage succeed. Sex alone is certainly not enough. Sex and love might get you through the night. But it takes sex, love, and God in common to make a marriage last through the years. Then, and only then, do the Lady, the Lover, and the Lord become a threefold cord strong enough to hold the relationship together.

> Again, if two lie down together, they will keep warm; but how can one be warm alone? Though one may be overpowered by another, two can withstand him. And a threefold cord is not quickly broken.
>
> Eccles. 4:11–12 (NKJ)

So, when you are choosing a companion, look for the man who is as related to you as a brother. Look for the one with whom you can communicate without words. He is the one who knows what you are. He knows what you are going to say before the words leave your lips. He knows what is in your heart because it is in his too. You were cut off the same material. You sense things about each other as twins do. He is your brother. Undoubtedly you will face challenges and problems in life, but you will seek solutions in the same place. You will both turn to your Father. This is how Adam and Eve endured Satan's efforts to destroy them. When they were threatened, when their future was in jeopardy, they resolved it by coming together as brother and sister before their Father.

> And the LORD God called unto Adam, and said unto him, Where art thou? And he said, I heard thy voice in the garden, and I was afraid, because I was naked; and I hid myself. And he said, Who told thee that thou wast naked? Hast thou eaten of the tree, whereof I commanded thee that thou shouldest not eat? And the man said, The woman whom thou gavest

to be with me, she gave me of the tree, and I did eat. And the LORD God said unto the woman, What is this that thou hast done? And the woman said, The serpent beguiled me, and I did eat.

Gen. 3:9–13

They sound like two children caught stealing cookies out of a cookie jar. They stand before the Father embarrassed and in trouble. But they were able to find resolution because they share the same life's philosophy. They are brother and sister. They are made from the same clay. The same Father who created Adam formed Eve. The one who connects him, connects her. In short, the same God he calls Father she calls Father also.

Adam and Eve were able to stand before their God and ask for forgiveness. They knew they had sinned. They shared the same rules, the same sense of right and wrong. A marriage can't survive if the partners don't embrace the same moral standards. How can you correct a marital problem if one of you doesn't think there's a problem?

Remember, you must marry your brother. And no matter how erotic your relationship becomes, be sure that you always let brotherly love continue. All other feelings will come and go like the ebbing tide of the ocean. Brotherly love endures. Passion rises and falls from day to day, moment to moment. It would not be natural to feel raging passion all the time. That's as unnatural as eating twenty-four hours a day. Lust is the gluttony of passion, and it usually indicates a brokenness that is trying to find healing through the wrong medicine. A healthy relationship has diversity. It continually changes. The one thing that gives it stability is that the relationship is built on friendship. Passion may come and go, hard times may make you falter, but through it all you are friends. The truth of the matter is we all will face conflict, but when we do, if we are joined by the same Father, we will easily be corrected.

Adam and Eve's relationship is not the only one in the Book of Genesis that reflects this concept.

> And yet indeed she is my sister; she is the daughter of my father, but not the daughter of my mother; and she became my wife.   Gen. 20:12

Abraham tried to deceive his host by saying his wife Sara was his sister. In fact, she was actually his half sister. (Although this would be frowned upon today, it was an acceptable practice at the time. The old Hebrew Bible characters always insisted that their sons marry from within the family bloodline because they knew the family was a strong bond that would perpetuate itself through the same faith and the same life philosophy.) But perhaps "she is the daughter of my father" also refers to the fact that she too is a child of God. Sara was Abraham's half sister by blood, but his sister in faith. She was his sister and his wife. Now, please do not misunderstand me; I am not suggesting that we literally marry our biological siblings. That would be incestuous and deplorable. I just want you to understand that from the beginning, the strongest, most enduring relationships were ones in which both partners were children of God.

Before we move on to other issues, I again want to impress upon you the truth about love and sex. It is simply this: sex is a mere shadow of love. True intimacy occurs when the body is spent and the affection continues. It is the bonding of hearts that gives the feeling of acceptance, not the tangling of flesh. We all want acceptance. To be able to be with another without worrying about having to perform or impress, to know that we're with a friend, that is truly being loved. Men especially need someplace where they can escape the demands of having to maintain an image. We long for a place to rest, rest from the pressure of constantly having to perform and be judged not on who we are but what we do. When we know that we are loved because of who we are, we become healthier in mind and more intimate in expression. Why? Because we are freed from the fear of rejection and loosed from the anxiety of having to perform. We are your husbands, your protectors, your lovers, but sometimes we want to laugh and just be as your brothers. So when we fail to impress as great husbands or perform as great lovers or become remiss as protectors, let us at least be secure in the knowledge that we will always be your brothers. When all else fails, let brotherly love continue.

Chapter Eight

Satin Sheets Slide

Have you ever seen the rich satin sheets that are draped invitingly across the beds in magazines and commercials? They look so inviting. They evoke sensuality, sexuality, and romance. Picture black satin sheets decorated with a single red rose. The scene seems to promise nights of unbridled passion. Satin sheets appear to promise erotic evenings similar to the ones we read about in romance novels.

Yet I bet that whoever created the first set of satin sheets could not have been a man. Although I'd be hard-pressed to find a guy who didn't like the feel of satin against his skin, most men would agree that satin is the worst possible material for love. Let me explain. Satin is cold in the winter; it holds absolutely no heat. In the summer, it will make you sweat because it does not breathe. It does not absorb moisture, and it wrinkles like linen. But the worst thing about it, from a male perspective, is that it makes you slide like a skater in an ice rink. Satin sheets are horrendous for the man who wants to be amorous to the woman he loves. They will make him look like a real klutz as he slips around.

Satin is fine for the woman if she likes the feeling of a silky material on her spine. She can lie in the lap of luxury. But if the man is going to stay afloat, he would do far better to have some plain cotton or flannel sheets. You see, ladies, satin might be pretty, but it destroys all semblance of balance and leaves you grabbing for the bedpost and groping for handfuls of mattress just to turn around in the sack, much less try an acrobatic feat of passion. It is amazing that something that looks so inviting could be so impractical. If you decide to bring your husband home a gift for Christmas, never, never bring him satin sheets. He might break his leg trying to roll over and get a kiss.

I guess that just goes to show you that what looks good to the eye isn't always as good as it appears. No man would have created those sheets, and if he did he would have quickly done a recall after one night of lying on them. It may be the look of love that we all want, but God knows we see through different eyes. We may see the same thing, but we see it from different perspectives. There's nothing wrong with having different viewpoints. In fact, it's natural. Men and women are different creatures with different needs. Neither viewpoint is better than the other; neither is more right. They're just different.

Problems begin to arise when we fail to communicate. A lady may give her husband a set of satin sheets. She loves him and wants to give him the finest, most luxurious, romantic gift. But when he's not happy with those sheets, she becomes hurt and angry at his lack of appreciation. What she should realize is that although she was trying to make her partner happy, she was giving him what she wanted rather than what he wanted. This is a common mistake. We tend to want to give our spouses what we like rather than what they like or need. To make a relationship work, you must realize that your partner's needs may be different from your own. It's something a lot of us forget to do. You fail to consider that there may be some things that work for you but drive him crazy. Then, when the relationship goes sour, there is a feeling of shock and betrayal. You worked so hard and gave so much, but you never saw it coming. Could it be possible that you were busy enjoying your satin sheets while the man beside you was silently praying he wouldn't slide out of the bed? Men are just as guilty as women in this, but men also contribute to this problem in a special way. It's one of the many mistakes men make: we are silent about too many things. We don't communicate our needs. Then, when they're not met, we become sullen and resentful. The woman is left confused because she tried to make things nice for us. She thought she was doing a good thing, giving us what we wanted. But we never told her what we wanted, so she was on her own and had to guess. She brought home the satin sheets, and we just slid out of bed.

We enter into the same bed, the same relationships, and the same task of life, but we enter from different perspectives. There are some things that a woman wouldn't know if a guy didn't tell her, and vice versa. I'll be the one guy breaking the silence and saying the secrets. No more being polite. We don't like the sheets, and we are falling out of the bed. And the sad thing is: we are losing good women who brought the sheets home only because they thought it would make us happy.

Some of you may be raising your eyebrows, startled by the language I'm using. Well, here we go, walking through the maze of appropriate Christian terminology to find a word that doesn't exasperate the sensitive-minded spiritualist and yet adequately describes the passion that should exude from the marital bed. One of the things that secretly frustrate some Christians and often alienate non-Christians is our incessant need to sound as though we are walking around with halos on our heads and harps in our hands. One of the valid points often made against Christians is that our message doesn't always seem relative. Like the sheets, it looks good but does it work right? Well, we know that Christianity works, but many times we have preached only half of the message.

> When the dead rise, they will neither marry nor be given in marriage; they will be like the angels in heaven.
> Mark 12:25 (NIV)

The message we preach is not just a prep class for the sweet everafter. It is a relevant message that gives direction for the nasty here and now. Christianity is for this world. It deals with marriages and relationships. Likewise, marriage is not for heaven; it is for earth. It is the earthly institution that emulates the spiritual union between Christ and the church. It is the passionate embracing of souls whose affection has reached the level of covenant and can be illustrated only in each other's arms. It is as the Bible describes a threefold cord. The three components are God, the groom, and the bride. I speak regarding Christian marriage: it is the coupling of two people who have agreed about who they are to each other and who they are in relationship to God.

They are husband and wife. They are lovers. A lover is more than a bed partner. Being lovers is being someone's place of habitation, recreation, and rest. Being lovers means that a couple has a directional focus that has centered them on the commitment to fulfill each other's needs. When I say needs, I don't necessarily mean sex. A need can be fulfilled with a touch or simply an exchange of tender words. But whatever the need, the place of fulfillment is the same. It is in her husband's arms that she finds happiness. It is his wife's humor that causes him to chuckle during the day. When a warm, glowing ember ignites in her thoughts and causes her face to flush, it is a memory of him too personal to be discussed but too powerful to be forgotten. In a marriage, a man and wife are partners, lovers, friends. It is a bond so powerful, so special, that it is meant to last forever.

The challenge is to find in reality what marriage is in design. An engineer would be summoned when a created piece of machinery fails to function according to its design. The manufacturer would never decide that the product was no good just because it failed to function correctly. The engineer would study the design and alter the materials until he had achieved the desired results. Yet we so easily scrap marriages that we have invested years in because of the slightest misalignment. We must remember that anything worth having is worth fighting for. Let's not permit ourselves to walk away from a wonderful relationship just because it's not working exactly as planned. Instead, let's try to figure out where the malfunction is. The blueprint for marriage is perfect; any problems with our relationships are due to human dysfunction. Let's try to keep our marriage aligned with the divine plan.

I believe the greatest flaw in most marriages can be attributed to the fact that when we are told those famous words "you must communicate," we are not told that we speak different languages. In order to achieve the harmonious sound of a concerted love ballad, we must take time to understand the diversity of the instrumentation. Simply said, men are far different from women, and we need to understand those differences. She is a harp to be gently stroked, and she responds to the skillful hands of a careful minstrel. He is a bugle, brassy and shiny, producing a strong sound of alarm. The music that comes from one is far different from the music that comes from the other. They must be orchestrated. We want to maintain our uniqueness but blend together as a team for lifelong bliss and love. So today, you and I are going to listen in at the confessional booth of love. We are going to walk through some Biblical principles looking for clues that will help us keep the music playing in perfect harmony.

The Superman Syndrome

I have observed that the man who is given billing as the aggressor is not truly aggressive all of the time. Most men are aggressive in the things that we feel comfortable with: earning a living, protecting our families, maintaining our manly image. However, when we feel vulnerable and unsure of ourselves, we tend to withdraw and shut down. You see, it is our masculine image that we are trying to protect. Whether real or imagined, most men feel that they are expected to be certain of everything and in control at all times. But when it comes to our hearts, we are not always in control of our feelings. And rather than risk exposing our fear, frustration, or need, we tend to camouflage our deepest thoughts by parading our strengths. Beneath the beating of the drums of our "I've got it together parade" is someone who needs desperately to feel safe enough to be vulnerable and honest.

Perhaps men could be intimate if we didn't go to bed dressed like Superman. Is there ever a time that we can just lie there next to you, touching you, loving you, and be Clark Kent? Of course there is. You know it, but we don't. Not knowing it may make us great performers, but after you've seen a few shows, boredom sets in. The pressure to perform is destroying the possibility of real intimacy. Some people's marriages are just a series of old reruns. Revival isn't just for church. It is for every area of our lives. Your drive for your career needs occasional revival. So does your relationship with your children, your spouse, or anything else. It is time for a revival of love in your home.

If we are going to have revival in our love life and our marriage, we as men need to find the right spot. Every revival needs a location. Where does the revival begin in a home that has become as bland as cold toast? We men need to go on an expedition to find the seat of our woman's passion, and she in turn should reciprocate. Every woman has a button that needs to be pushed to guarantee her passion and fulfillment. It may not be where you think it is. I am convinced that the woman's special spot is in her heart. It is there that her nerve centers flash lights and honk horns. If you really want to make your lady sing, you better touch that special place.

Likewise, a man needs to be stroked from within. Unfortunately, he doesn't know how to ask for it. Sometimes he doesn't even know what is missing. He may not be adept enough at problem solving to tell her that he needs cotton sheets. He just knows that he is miserable sliding around in this satin sheet syndrome. So instead of communicating his needs, he medicates the problem rather than healing the cause. Generally he gets high on his job or illegal drugs, or he goes on a sexual marathon. He just keeps looking for mo' money, mo' sex, and mo' power. I taught a class called "P.M.S." P.M.S. was an acronym for power, money, and sex. Damaged men run to these things for solace when we slide off the sheets of a relationship. It's where we go when we can't maintain the position we need. But we don't really need the money, the power, or the sex; what we need is to be rocked in the cradle of a loving woman's arms, a woman who knows how to make the sliding stop.

Superman needs a nap. He needs to take off his cape and boots and relax in the arms of Lois Lane. But the man is wondering, "Will she like me when the cape is gone?" Not only can the right lady allow a man to rest, she can make a man feel comfortable doing it. He can trust her and let down his guard. No wonder the Bible says that whosoever findeth a good wife findeth a good thing. The right lady is a "good thing" to a man who has seen too many bad things. The plain truth is this: the big guy may be mighty in the boardroom, in the courtroom, or on the football field, but sometimes he feels like a little boy inside and needs the soft touch of your loving embrace.

For Most Men, Loving Is Easier Than Trusting!

> The heart of her husband doth trust safely in her, so that he shall have no need of spoil.   Prov. 31:11

A man needs a good wife, whom he can trust with his heart. He needs to be able to place it with her and know it will not flutter or shake if it is in her firm embrace. With the right woman, his heart has found its place of rest. It curls up in her like a bear hibernating for the winter. She is warm to him. She is safe. Her gentle fragrance is the aroma he sleeps in and the fragrance he awakes to. His heart is in her like a baby in a blanket. When love is right, he finds in her what he could not find in others. She is in a class so alone that she has no contenders. She has his rhythm and hears his beat. She dances to the beating of his heart, and he sways to the pulsing in her veins. They are music together!

Trust is the greatest struggle for most men. They often find it difficult to rely on anyone other than themselves. The male heart is generally guarded and locked down with intense security. Yet even though the heart is protected so securely, it is still fragile when it comes to trust and love. A man's heart is as fragile as the tender shell of an unhatched egg. Trust is the root of love for a man. Where there is no trust, love has no place to be nourished. Trust is the root from which love is nourished.

There are several areas of trust that are essential for a man to feel whole and fulfilled.

1. He needs to trust her motives.

When a man trusts his wife, he is at peace in her presence and seeks refuge in her arms. This trust is deeper than the confidence in the validity of her words. It embraces a sense of confidence that reaches even into her intentions. When I speak of him trusting her, I am speaking in regard to his need to feel certain of her motives and sure of her values. You see, most men do not understand their wife's methods, so if he doesn't trust her motives, he has nothing left to trust in. The female methods are so different from men's. They think differently. They react differently. And the only way a man can endure the difference is by feeling secure that her motives are as clear as mountain water. If he begins to question her motives while he is already confused by her methods, he withdraws immediately. He needs to know that her focus is fixed in his direction.

If a man loses trust in his wife, he will immediately shut down and withdraw. He will be unresponsive to her tears, her affections, and all her efforts at closeness. He becomes suspicious of her motives and cautious in her presence. Once trust is lost, it takes so long to regain it because a man won't let his guard down long enough to let the woman into his heart again. Trust needs to be handled like a fragile treasure. Its value is great, but it is easily broken. Preserve the trust; a relationship cannot last without it.

2. He needs to be able to trust her sexually.

A man needs to know that his wife wants him and him alone. Few men are comfortable with a woman who has a roving eye. Perhaps it is the stereotype we have causing us to feel that when a woman's eye roves it generally means her heart has long since wandered away. But that is not the only area where a man needs to trust her sexually. He needs to know that what goes on in their bed is not the subject of conversation at her girlfriend's house. He needs to know, when he pleases her or does not please her, that she is satisfied to discuss it only with him. He needs to know that his woman is discreet. Finally, he needs to be able to believe her reactions. He needs to know that her response is not created for his entertainment. If she deceives him about her pleasure, he cannot trust her and he shrinks away inside. Her acting is painful because it not only makes him feel inadequate, it also makes him feel like he is being tampered with, and he feels as though his intelligence is being discredited.

3. He needs to trust her not to change.

> Husbands, likewise, dwell with them with understanding, giving honor to the wife, as to the weaker vessel, and as being heirs together of the grace of life, that your prayers may not be hindered.   I Pet. 3:7 (NKJ)

This level of trust encompasses areas of the relationship that are far more nebulous and difficult to articulate. The man wants a woman he can trust to be consistent the same way a traveler seeks a compass that will not change its direction or a clock that will not alter its time. The changing woman terrifies the man. He lives in fear that she will change on him in the middle of a crisis. Often he doesn't understand her changes. Most men are confused by the ever-changing presentation of their wives. She cries without warning. She asks questions and then gets irritated when he answers. He thinks that she is discussing problems to get an answer. He doesn't know that she asks questions to vent frustration. He doesn't realize that she just wants to be heard. He tries to help her by offering solutions, and she gets annoyed because she didn't want an answer. She wanted an ear. These changes are intimidating to most men.

The cause of women's changes may be biological. Hormonal fluctuations due to menstruation, menopause, or pregnancy can cause women to change dramatically. But even if these changes are natural, they still leave men confused. We are commanded to dwell with the lady according to our understanding. But the honest confession of most men is that they generally do not understand women. It is hard to live with someone whom you do not understand. If the woman is to gain the trust of her mate, she must be able to explain herself to him. "I am not angry at you, honey, I am going through a physical change right now that might affect me." He can deal with what he understands. It is what he doesn't understand that destroys trust.

The woman is a strange species to a man. She is an odd combination of strength and weaknesses, fears and tears. Yes, her difference makes her alluring and intriguing, but she can also seem as foreign as an alien. She is some strange novel that he reads with fascination. She is a mystery unfolding in his arms. Sometimes he thinks he knows exactly what she needs, and then she seems to transform right before his very eyes. This can cause the man to become suspicious and introverted. Men are like turtles in that if they sense danger, they retract into a shell for safety. A man can physically be with a woman but have moved away from her emotionally. Many women do not know that the lover they sleep with is a man who has left home in his mind. It is possible for either partner to retract into a shell while the other is oblivious to the withdrawal. Because men are so noncommunicative by nature, it is more common that a man can retract into a shell and not discuss it. His body is in the bed, but his heart is hidden for fear of rejection, pain, frustration, or secret resentment.

4. He needs to trust her not to use his openness against him later.

Because it is difficult for most men to open up, they are very watchful to see the after-effects of their openness. If he finally gets the courage to open up to you, you must be careful not to use his moment of openness against him later. If you do, he will never trust you with his innermost thoughts again. His little pearls of truth are not to be cast before the swine. And do not try to psycho-analyze him. He will feel overexposed and withdraw. When he does share his feelings with you, be careful not to intensify them. If he tells you how he feels about his mother and father, don't you speak badly of them. He may have just needed to vent his frustration. Your criticism of them may hurt his feelings and place his loyalty in conflict. When he opens up to you, sometimes your silence will create the greatest impact. A loving nod, a touch, a few words, and a kiss are the most effective response. If you want to establish trust, just listen to him.

> For thus saith the Lord GOD, the Holy One of Israel; . . . in quietness and in confidence shall be your strength: and ye would not. Isa. 30:15

5. He needs to trust her not to be in competition with him.

The challenge that most men have with a successful woman erupts when her success overshadows the relationship and excludes him. He needs to know that she still finds him fit to lead in some areas, even if she excels in others. It is not wise to compete with your mate. Whenever that happens, no one wins. We all lose because the partnership is devoured by the competition and the marriage is dissolved.

One way competition can be avoided is to support one another mutually. Real love always builds up the other person. Now granted, some people are so dysfunctional that building them up is like building a sand castle too close to the water. No matter how you build them, they will soon be washed away by the next current. A man so insecure should never marry a woman who is on a mission with her career. He will never be able to handle it. But even the more stable man will become weary if he is made to feel that he is being constantly measured or compared against her success. Sometimes he is made to feel he is competing with a father's or ex-husband's success. It does not matter whose success it is; what matters is that he feels he is being measured against it.

Many men may be reluctant to share these worries with a woman, but rest assured, most men would agree with them. If a lady will heed these points, trust will be established. Now, some of you may be thinking, "I have already violated trust and didn't even realize that I had done it." I know how you feel. All of us have made mistakes that we didn't mean to, or want to, make. But we all have the opportunity to rectify previous mistakes. If you are a concerned wife who wants to change her methods, you have been armed with the helpful hints that will enable you to experience the complete restoration of trust in your relationship. Armed with these tools, you will encourage your husband to move gradually from being the strong, silent type toward becoming a man who opens his heart and shares his innermost thoughts, and your life will be richer with each other.

I have shared these ideas with you not to suggest blame, but to teach you the language of men, so you can converse with openness and honesty. A marriage is a collaboration of two hearts that join together to overcome the obstacles of life and create an atmosphere of shared pleasure and deeper love. If you can't agree on the sheets, then go for the plain mattress. But whatever it takes, make it happen for both of you.

Chapter Nine

Pillow Talk

Yᴏᴜ shall have whatever you say.
Mark 11:23

These powerful words are extracted out of a lesson that Jesus the great teacher shared with his disciples about the power of the spoken word. It is fitting that a God who created the earth by the power of his words would then teach his disciples to be careful of what they say.

And God said, Let there be light: and there was light.   Gen. 1:3

It is in the same spirit that I share with

you the extreme power that exists when you use your tongue for good or for evil in your own house and relationship. Those who would idly say whatever they want without awareness of consequences are sadly naïve. Many of us have been the victim of hateful, thoughtless words, and we have been bruised by them. Most of us are living with the consequences of our own speech—whether it was a "yes" given too hastily or an opinion shared too quickly. We enter into relationships with our mouths open, even if our eyes are closed. Many of you have said things that bruised your companion and changed the tenor of your relationship. If your mouth got you in the troubled relationship that you are in, then theoretically it stands to reason that your mouth can get you out. The injury can be healed, but saying "I am sorry" is not always enough. Those magic words are not nearly as healing as the statements that led to them are damaging. But with a careful rebuilding of credibility through controlled speech, you can regain what you lost through the abuse of the tongue.

A woman needs to understand the effect her words have on a man's performance; her words can motivate or disintegrate his self-esteem. In fact, the words of a woman can influence a man more than anything else. Think about it: We live in a matriarchal society. Most men talk to their mothers more openly than to their fathers. It is the mother that the young football player speaks to as he looks into the camera after making the winning touchdown. Men have often been encouraged by the feminine voice. As a child, it was a woman's voice that scolded and corrected them. It was a woman's voice that sang them to sleep when they were afraid of the dark. More often than not, a feminine voice taught him in school. A wife's voice is just as powerful to an adult man. If that voice is adversarial and complaining, it affects his persona. On the other hand, a word of encouragement can renew his desire to survive.

The Bible teaches us that the power of life and death is in the tongue. A woman who speaks comfortably and carefully to a man can encourage a greater strength and courage than one who is consistently confrontational. Her words can exalt him or demolish him. She can say things that make him want to retreat to the rooftop rather than to be close to her. No one realizes the power of words as much as preachers. Preaching is just the coordinating of words with an intent to build up and direct. Every major revolution in history was accomplished by someone who knew what to say. Anyone, male or female, who recklessly spurts out words is speaking death to their relationship.

> It is better to live in a corner of the roof than in a house shared with a contentious woman.
>
> Prov. 25:24 (NAS)

The man flees from contention but draws strength from the woman who encourages him and affirms him. But that is not unique to the male species. Any of us will draw closer to the warm voice of affirmation more quickly than we would to the shrill voice of constant criticism. Calm spirits create trust and tranquillity. This is the key to long-lasting relationships. It is in this environment that positive change and development can best be accomplished. Even if there are areas that desperately need to be changed, hostility will not bring about change; it will just result in resentment and hiding his heart on the roof. You can keep your lover off the roof and in the bed with tenderness.

A woman who knows what to say is a

mighty powerful force. She can influence her husband. Not only can she strengthen him and give him courage, she can motivate him. Men react to praise as God reacts to praise. David says that God is magnified through spoken praise.

> O magnify the LORD with me, and
> let us exalt his name together.
>
> Ps. 34:3

This psalm uses the term "magnify," which literally means to cause to grow. When we praise God he increases in our lives. Any man who is praised will begin to grow. Men always try to impress women who fuss over them. If a woman seems impressed by a guy who carries two bags of groceries and still unlocks the door, he will grab three bags and say to her, "Check this out! No problem, it's a piece of cake." He will say it even if he is out of breath and delirious. Her words motivate him to perform.

That is how children are positively motivated. Encouragement yields results. Men react to words. Watch a little boy who is spoken well of. Watch him try even harder to impress. The voice of a woman has caused the little boy in us to try harder in all we do. It has given us courage to fight the giants in our lives.

It is that same feminine voice that can cause men to grow. A woman who knows what to say can make a man drop his newspaper in the chair and spend the evening in her arms. It is the power of the spoken word that moves men. It will move a man forward or it will demolish him. It just depends on what words are said to him. There are things a woman can say to a man that crush him so terribly that he is impotent. Her words can make him impotent sexually, spiritually, or economically. There is power that erupts from the feminine voice. If that power is directed for good, it will motivate him in every area.

Yes, a woman's words spoken sweetly can greatly influence a man. Even Jesus performed a miracle prior to His plan because Mary, His mother, came to Him and asked Him for help. Her looking to Him was so compelling that He turned water into wine.

> And the third day there was a marriage in Cana of Galilee; and the mother of Jesus was there: And both Jesus was called, and his disciples, to the marriage. And when they wanted wine, the

mother of Jesus saith unto him, They have no wine. Jesus saith unto her, Woman, what have I to do with thee? mine hour is not yet come. His mother saith unto the servants, Whatsoever he saith unto you, do it. And there were set there six waterpots of stone, after the manner of the purifying of the Jews, containing two or three firkins apiece. Jesus saith unto them, Fill the waterpots with water. And they filled them up to the brim. And he saith unto them, Draw out now, and bear unto the governor of the feast. And they bare it. When the ruler of the feast had tasted the water that was made wine, and knew not whence it was (but the servants which drew the water knew) the governor of the feast called the bridegroom, And saith unto him, Every man at the beginning doth set forth good wine; and when men have well drunk, then that which is worse: but thou hast kept the good wine until now.   John 2:1–10

If your relationship has lost the sweet taste of wine and has become the dismal waters of mundane routine, try speaking gently to him. You'd be surprised what a wedding night can be derived from a woman who knows how to speak to her husband. There is still a carafe of Chablis left in his heart for you. Speak softly to him, and get ready to say that God has saved the best wine for last.

Study the power of the tongue. Understand that if the power is not bridled it can be dangerous to any relationship.

> So also the tongue is a small part of the body, and [yet] it boasts of great things. Behold how great a forest is set aflame by such a small fire! And the tongue is a fire, the [very] world of iniquity; the tongue is set among our members as that which defiles the entire body, and sets on fire the course of [our] life, and is set on fire by hell.
>
> James 3:5–6 (TLB)

It is amazing to think that something so small can destroy relationships, ruin opportunities, damage children, cripple women, and emasculate men. Yet I tell you the truth. More people are hurt by a tongue out of control than by any gun. It is small, it is quick, and it is deadly. The worst part of it is that we tend to use it most effectively against those who are vulnerable enough to care what we say. Your real enemies will never be wounded by your words because they will never dignify your words with their attention. It is the people who love you and want to be with you who are most likely to become assaulted by your words. One day you will look into their eyes and notice that you have doused the fire that once burned inside them. It was your tongue that did it. Please stop it before you murder your friend, your career, your child, or your companion!

All of us who are quick-witted have to harness our tongue. Can you imagine what would happen if everyone said everything that they thought? Just because you know what to say to lame a person does not mean that you have the right to say it. Before you speak, weigh the effects of your words. You may not be able to retract them. So be sure that you mean them before you hurl them at someone tonight whom you may want to love you tomorrow.

Sadly, though, most people who have never learned to bridle their tongues end up alone, for everyone who would have been there has been lashed away by a tongue that could not be controlled. The children leave, the husband escapes, and the employers don't give promotions. And the worse things get, the more brutal the tongue becomes. The more brutal the tongue gets, the greater the alienation becomes. It's a vicious cycle. Can you see yourself in these lines? If so, ask God to give you the grace to use your tongue for good and not evil. If you will allow Him, He will take your tongue and direct it for His glory rather than your destruction.

Here is a good prayer for you to pray if you feel that you are struggling in this area. Harboring a knife under your pillow really destroys pillow talk for you and the one you love. Get rid of that dagger by addressing it in prayer. Simply ask God for His harness over your tongue.

> Let the words of my mouth, and the
> meditation of my heart, be acceptable
> in thy sight, O LORD, my strength,
> and my redeemer.   Ps. 19:14

Your mouth is designed to speak blessings and petition heaven. You are meant to see your prayers answered. You have been given a swift tongue, so you can speak peace to storms and life to the dead things that arise against you. The evil one has no right to use what God gave you, but the devil is trying to use it to destroy you. I want you to make the commitment to change your speech into something wholesome. If you do, when you are old you will be surrounded by people who want to hear you speak.

When in love, your mouth is filled with an elixir mixed from the honey of your thoughts and the wine of your affections. When you speak, the sound of your voice should stir passion in your mate and not be associated with pain. There are women who have been able to walk into a room and speak a word that causes their husbands to awake out of unconsciousness. I remember a man I knew who had a terrible accident and slipped into a coma. The doctors had given up all hope, but his wife never did. She kept speaking to him. In fact, she kept praying for him. He later said her voice was in his ears calling him back from the light. It was not only a strong prayer that pulled him through; it was a familiar voice that made him climb out of the arms of death. When you speak, you can call men from a state of depression or despair. You have the power; use it for good. If you do, you will be a rich woman all of your life. You will be rich in friends, rich in success, and rich in admiration. Men deeply appreciate a woman who is full of kind words.

As I close this issue there is one thing that I want you to know. If you are going to enjoy a wholesome relationship, there must be communication between you and your mate. But there is a difference between discussing and resolving a conflict through communicating and unleashing hellfire on someone with your lethal tongue. Resolve conflict, but do not abuse each other with words. They are so easily spoken, but they are difficult to erase. Use your words to share your dreams and needs and to ask your lover what he wants. We see things from different perspectives. If you give him only what you like, it will cause great frustration partially because your intentions were so sincere and yet your efforts did not elicit the proper response. Secondly, it frustrates him because giving is only effective when we humble ourselves enough to allow the other person's needs or desires to take precedence over our own biases and preferences. You may have to climb into the bed together while the children are fast asleep and talk. Yes, that's right, just talk. Talk until the morning light peeks into the window. Talk until the robin chirps its early-morning song of daybreak. This is your life you are fighting to save. Without communication, your relationship will surely die, and with it the promise of love and comfort for all your days on earth.

So what's a girl to do? you ask. I suggest that while you lie in your bed or drive together to work, you always develop the art of communication. Sometimes you will speak in words, other times words won't be necessary. There are times you can speak volumes without opening your mouth. Your hands and eyes can often send louder messages if they're used the right way. But no matter how you speak, just be sure that you do speak. Communication will help you maintain an understanding of each other's needs. Negotiate your needs so that everyone wins. Your job is to bring joy into each other's life. There is never anything wrong with someone asking, "How can I make your life better?" Just asking the question means a lot. The consideration it implies makes the person feel loved and appreciated.

So I'm prescribing a large dose of communication—a few hours of touch, followed by a generous application of eye contact. And every night, before you go to sleep, whisper something in each other's ear that makes you need to wrap up in each other. A good relationship feels like a warm blanket on a cold night. Cuddle up close and insulate yourself from the events of the day. Reach over in the night for the warm place in each other's heart and then, ever so softly, whisper your pillow talk.

Chapter Ten

Make Him Feel Safe Enough to Love You

It seems crazy that a big, strong man needs to feel secure, but he does. He needs it in the worst way. He can be terribly afraid and confused by feminine behavior. We always resent what we do not understand, and there are many things between the genders that we often do not understand. Trust is a major area of concern for both parties. A countless number of books and magazine articles have explored trust from a female perspective as it relates to infidelity. But there seems to be a real dearth of material that helps the woman understand the masculine need to trust in a woman and feel safe. What complicates the issue further is the fact that most men do not discuss their feelings easily. Much of a man's uneasiness may be due to his experience in past relationships, either his own or ones that he witnessed as a child. He may have observed that opening oneself up emotionally creates vulnerability. He may have experienced the pain himself when he shared his feelings only to have them thrown back in his face in a moment of rage. He will not always readily supply the reason for his silence, even when he is repeatedly admonished to discuss himself. Sometimes he is silent because he doesn't even know the cause. Or he just might not realize the effect his wary attitude and sullen habits have on you.

Developing trust is difficult for a man. And when he finally does trust, and that trust is betrayed, he may lock himself in a vault of silence and never come out. Trust is hard enough to win in the first place, but if you give a man cause to feel you have violated his trust, it may be impossible to win it back. I cannot tell you how many men have confided in me that they don't trust their women. They love their women, but don't trust them. Many men feel that women manipulate them with words, so in their own defense, men remain silent. But realize that his silence does not indicate his assent. It just indicates that he has lapsed further from you than he was before. The unique thing about men is that most of them have the ability to be sexually intimate and still remain emotionally distant. Do not think that his amorous aggression in bed is always a barometer that correctly indicates his wholeness within himself or his relationship.

For a man, trust is feeling assured that no matter what changes she incurs as she evolves through life, his position in her life will not be threatened. It is knowing that she will not deceive him. It is being sure that she will be his friend forever. Trust is the issue that haunts a man's heart. Often, the insecurity that causes men to be terrified of commitment is associated with trust. It's not that they want to remain single so much as it is a fear of having to trust someone. They're so afraid of being hurt that they would rather be alone. Some men were raised not to trust women. Sound strange? Well, many men have grown up in homes where they have seen or heard too much. These boys have heard the discussions that disgruntled women have about men, and it leaves them confused. Many men are scarred by broken childhoods filled with broken memories. They have seen the conflicts, heard the screaming, and been torn apart.

No matter how justified the conflict may be between the mother and the father, the child should never have to hear his mother speak evil of his father. It causes distrust in him as he feels that a covenant between two people has been violated, and he loses respect for the bond of marriage. Whatever problems you may have with the father, do not use the son to vent your frustrations or as a weapon in a war between you and your mate. The son who is split apart emotionally may not act out his confusion on you, but when he is older he will struggle to trust his wife. He has seen betrayal in his own mother, and if he can't trust her, what woman can he trust?

> I am not speaking [this] as a command, but as proving through the earnestness of others the sincerity of your love also. For you know the grace of our Lord Jesus Christ, that though He was rich, yet for your sake He became poor, that you through His poverty might become rich.
>
> II Cor. 8:8–9 (NAS)

When a man loves, he is vulnerable in a way that is threatening to himself. Even God, when He loves us, becomes poor. That literally means that love spends its resources in caring. We enrich the one we love, but we do it by spending ourselves on them. Most men are intimidated by the expense of an emotional commitment. Oh yes, he wants the benefits, but he may be afraid of the bill!

Men tend to feel uncertain with their own feelings. We have had little practice at relationships. We never grew up playing house. While girls played with wedding gowns and dressed Barbie and Ken for marriage, guys were playing with army tanks and games that did not prepare them for relationships. While little girls played with dolls that needed blankets and changing and feeding, little boys played with trains that did not require much emotion. In short, men are "thing" oriented. We are better at handling things than we are at handling people. Especially when the people have needs that are so different from our own.

It is far easier for him to give his money, his body, his advice, but when he gives his heart, then he is terrified. What will you do to me if I need you? If I allow myself to open up, what will come out of my heart?

he wonders. Suddenly, even the most robust man trembles when he knows that he has gone beyond wanting her to needing her. Wanting is safe, but needing is vulnerable. He feels as though his heart is held in her hand, but he fears that the hand will become an iron fist to crush him and leave him hurting. When thoughts of her cause moisture to gather in his eyes and thunder to beat wildly in his heart, a man begins to worry. He feels vulnerable, exposed. He feels naked in the tempestuous storm of love. What he doesn't realize is that a woman's love is a shelter, protection from the wind. Open your arms and your heart to him. Show him he's safe; let him come out of the cold.

Home Alone

And the LORD God called unto Adam, and said unto him, Where art thou? And he said, I heard thy voice in the garden, and I was afraid, because I was naked; and I hid myself.
Gen. 3:9–10

If God Himself had to ask man, "Where are you?" then surely you can see that our whole society, from fatherless children to husbandless wives, is echoing the same valid question. You know that you do not have to be single to be alone. You can be in a relationship and still be on your own. A man can lie in the bed with you and still be hiding. He can provide for you financially and come home in the evening and flop down in a chair and still not be there. Women are so instinctive that they generally know when they are truly left home alone. But even when she senses that he is not there, she often doesn't know where he is. The worst part is that she may not know how to get him back.

Adam hid when he was threatened, and men still hide today. Some men hide behind a macho attitude that suggests they are indifferent and not really participating. They spend all of their lives acting like little boys, playing with leftover childhood toys: sports, golf, job contracts, cars, gambling, etc. These are the toys of our childhood reincarnated. My brother once told me that the only difference between men and boys is how much they pay for their toys. But understand that the toys are not always an indication of childishness. It is man avoiding the uncharted waters of emotional honesty. It is a hiding that is done out of insecurity, which could be healed by a strong dose of trust. Some men hide behind their jobs; others hide behind sex. They chase women as a hobby rather than to risk having a relationship. They are afraid of taking the relationship too seriously. They are little boys who dehumanize women to toy status, so they can feel safe with them rather than deal with a mutually satisfying relationship.

Love is not a monologue; it is a dialogue. It is a dialogue that occurs between two people who do not know what the other's response will be. It is hard to prepare for a conversation when you cannot predict the response of the other person. It is that unpredictability that causes some men to feel uncomfortable and afraid. You'd be surprised at the emotional state of some men who come home from work carrying bad news. They are filled with anxiety over having to tell their wife what happened. Now, this guy is a two-hundred-forty-eight-pound hunk of lead. He has bulging biceps, and he looks like Mr. Atlas. If he were facing a man, he would walk in with total control, but there he is driving home, dreading having to tell his one-hundred-thirty-pound wife that he has done this or that. It is not her size that makes him vulnerable. It is her importance to him.

Sadly, she may not even realize the status she has in his heart. Often, he does not know how to tell her that she is that important to him. He doesn't even want her to know that he drove around the block three extra times preparing how he was going to tell her what he has to say. The plain truth is he doesn't trust her response to him, or he does not feel safe.

It is this uncertainty that keeps a man from saying too much, getting too close. Who knows how she'll respond? Yes, spontaneity is exciting. An unexpected kiss, a free-flowing dance—the unknown can be thrilling. But what happens if he kisses a head that turns or dances with a partner who suddenly, rigidly refuses to respond? The uncertainty of the future is as frightening to a man as a pit bull is to a feline!

A man struggles to trust a woman. Are her words really conveying what her heart feels? When he is making love to her, is she really enraptured or just accommodating? The more he can know her, the easier he can share his heart, his secrets, and his scars with her. Now, none of us is afraid to tell anyone anything that we think they will approve of. The real test is to talk when what we have to say is embarrassing or negative. And how much more challenging for a man to say these things to the woman he loves! If love had not caught him, he would have no need to be intimidated. But the more he loves and needs a woman, the more unsure of himself he is. He wonders, if she knew how much he needed her, would she still see him as a strong man? What would happen if he came home and cried in her arms for once? He doesn't know that in most cases a woman would love to have a man who was comfortable enough with her to be vulnerable. The lady is tired of dealing with men who wrap themselves up in protective armor. She can't get close to a man like that and doesn't want to keep trying to touch him through a thick metal shield. She wants to touch his heart, his need, and even his fear. It is that degree of nakedness that reassures her his love is real. If she doesn't get that, she keeps asking questions. Questions that drive men crazy. Questions such as, "Do you love me? I mean do you really love me?"

Conversely, men think women are impenetrable. A man will stare at a woman with the wide-eyed wonder of a child. She is as lovely as a picture in a museum, but she is surrounded by glass that keeps him from touching her. This glass is the feminine personality. It is her mood changes, her defense mechanisms that she uses to protect herself from a world that is not always fair and accepting, her own coat of armor that she wears so men cannot hurt her as they did in the past. This glass case around a woman keeps a man uncertain, and he finds it nearly impossible to break through to the soul mate on the other side of his uncertainty. So you have two people, both wrapped up and protected, but insulated and unable to touch each other. No wonder relationships are so difficult. Have you ever noticed that there are some couples who get along better after they are separated than when they were together? Sadly, they gave up on a marriage, not because what they needed wasn't there. It's more likely that they could not find a way to penetrate the wrapping and get to the contents of each other's hearts. They are still in love with each other; it is just that they found themselves angry at being so close and yet so very, very far.

Matters of the Heart

The silent, often sullen man sits gazing out of a window or down into a glass. He is locked in the chambers of his own thoughts, oblivious to what occurs around him. Like a juror, he ponders a verdict with great deliberation. He ponders whether she is a safe and credible witness for him to open his heart before. His heart has generally been sealed like a vault and covered with cobwebs. To attempt to open it is a challenging task. He often offers her things in substitution for his heart, as it is easier for him to give substance rather than self. These trinkets of affection are meant to appease her and convey affection without endangering the real treasure of their relationship, which is his heart.

Most men do not associate the giving of their body with the giving of their heart, but women tend to tie the two together. A woman generally offers her body only when she is ready to offer her heart. The giving of her body epitomizes her commitment to her partner. It signifies that she is in love. The virtuous woman values herself too much to be passed around from man to man. Her body generally comes to the altar of love only when there is a safe sense of affection. She will give herself physically only when she is ready to give herself spiritually. Whenever she offers her body, it is an indication that her heart is somewhere close. Yes, her heart lies trembling on the altar; her body is just an announcement that she is serious about her significant other. It signifies her intent to continue the relationship. This is true passion. This is true love. It cannot be demanded or paid for. It comes only when the woman gives it freely and on her own terms. The body and the heart combine to form an elixir, the sweetest wine anyone will ever taste. It is the intoxicating experience that causes a silly grin to emerge on the face of a man in the middle of the day. It is what makes the woman blush and sigh softly at her desk. Yes, when a virtuous woman gives her body, she is also giving her heart and soul. What a treasure to behold!

It is tragic that there are women who have sunk into the abyss of deplorable lust without love. These women are usually the victims of an unhealthy upbringing and traumatic experiences that left them wounded and with low self-esteem. They don't value themselves, and thus give their bodies away to anyone who asks. Or else they use their bodies because they think it is the only way they can get a man. They think their bodies are the only things they have to barter with in the game of love. But love is not a game, nor can it be traded. When a woman gives herself too easily, she loses worth in the eyes of men. If she doesn't value herself, why should they? But when a woman knows that her body and her heart are two jewels in the same crown, she will give that crown only to a man who is worthy. She should give it only to a prince.

Most women do place a high value on the giving of their body, and thus believe in monogamy. To them, infidelity is an unforgivable sin. Most women see adultery as the epitome of betrayal. To them, sex and love are not mutually exclusive. But often, this is not the mentality of men. Unfortunately, all too many men have proven that they have the capacity to have their affections in one place and their sexual energies in another. You see, men find it easy to give their bodies; it is the giving of their hearts that is difficult for them. A young man may be very eager to fondle his date, but be terrified to make a commitment that would require him to offer his heart. If she asks him to promise undying sex, he would do it in a heartbeat. But if she asks him to promise undying love, he would stagger backward in fear. He goes around having sex and thinking he's getting love. It feels good, and he's not emotionally vulnerable. What he doesn't realize is that he's only getting half of the pie, and he's missing the best part. So he keeps having sex without sharing his heart, wondering why he's not satisfied. So to find satisfaction, he has even more sex. This becomes a huge problem when the man is married. He says he loves his wife, but he's afraid to give her his heart. Then, when he feels the marriage is missing something, he looks outside for fulfillment. The sad part is he often doesn't realize he is doing something wrong.

When a man is unfaithful, he will seldom confess. Generally, he has to get caught. Even when he is caught red-handed, he often will try to lie his way out of it. The woman is irate with an anger that many men do not understand. She feels cheap and dirty. She often feels that she has failed and that somehow his problem is an indication she is not enough. She is humiliated and feels betrayed. When she confronts him, she attacks him with venomous insults and raging tears. She almost always says, "How could you?" He usually stands there looking like a three-year-old who got caught with his hand in the cookie jar. He almost always says, "It's not what it looks like." Then, to make it even worse, he says, "It was just sex. But I love you!" By then she is ready to kill him. She doesn't understand him. If he loves her, he would have come home last night! Is she right? Yes, she is right to expect commitment from her husband. Why then is he standing there looking confused? Could he love her and still be unfaithful? Yes. Think about it. We, as Christians, love the Lord but we are often unfaithful to Him. He expects us to be committed and faithful, doesn't He? Have you ever broken your vow to Him? And does He forgive us? Yes.

Most Christian women who have been taught anything at all about mercy will wrestle long over this because, whether we admit it or not, we all have done foolish things that did not reflect our real heart and values. There is a point when you know that this man will never change and he has no repentance in him. But it is dangerous to refuse to forgive a truly repentant person, no matter who they are and what they did. You might later have to reap the rigidity of your own judgment. This is what the Scripture suggests when it declares, "With what measures you mete it will be mete unto you." Your infraction may not be in the same area of weakness, but we have all dealt with regret over foolish character flaws. The God who knows us intimately often watches

212

how we deal out judgment when we finally get the advantage of being right. Power can be a real test of character. How do you handle mercy when you feel justified to condemn? Keep this in mind as you sentence your husband.

I know that there is a place of no return and sadly there may be marriages that are fatally afflicted, but not all of them that are going to court need to go there. Some of them need to go to the altar, where the vows were originally made, and ask God for grace to help them change and heal. Yes, it is a terrible weakness in his character, but weaknesses can be healed. You must decide. Yes, you can walk away and say, "You failed and I quit." Maybe you should. Each case is different. The decision belongs to you. But do not rule out forgiveness too quickly. It may be possible that your relationship can be resurrected. Look into your husband's eyes and you may see that he doesn't mean to hurt you; he just needs to be taught how to be faithful. Pray to God for the strength to forgive him and the patience to teach him. Realize that you must be strong enough to demand to be respected, but gentle enough to allow your mate the grace to grow. Should you stay or should you go? Ultimately the decision is your own. Make your choice carefully. Allow the Lord to lead you.

> Blessed are the merciful: for they shall
> obtain mercy.   Matt. 5:7

The real truth is that unless men are consistently told and shown that love and sex are inseparable, they generally will not be conditioned to respect sex as a sign of commitment. Hopefully we are changing that in how we raise this next generation. But for now, we must try to teach men that the body and heart must go together.

I know that what I have said about men are generalizations and that there are exceptions. But I share these things to show you the difference between men and women. Ladies, the most important thing for you to realize now is how guarded men keep their hearts. Understand that he wants to share himself, but he is afraid. If he is to get the courage to unlock the vault of his affections, he will require a great price: nothing short of absolute trust. What is trust in marriage? I am glad you asked. It deserves repeating.

For a man to trust in his wife, it means that he is not inhibited in her presence. He has examined her thoughts, and he knows that they are in sync with his own. In her arms, he is all things he cannot be with others. In her arms, he is a giant, a warrior, a protector. In her arms, he is a lamb looking for shelter against the storm. He is strong and fierce. He is a whimpering, trembling child. In her arms, he is commanding and sure. In her arms, he is looking for peace and reassurance. He is holding her and being held by her. It is the kind of trust that enables him to whisper his deepest fears in her ears and tell his darkest secrets. The woman he trusts is too wise to laugh and too concerned to condemn him. She will not betray his confidence, discuss his secrets, or air his weaknesses. She will not speak ill of him nor agree with his enemies in public. She is on his side. Oh yes, she is his rib. She is connected to him. He trusts her in his heart, and she is there for him in the crises of life.

To be sure, a woman who can be trusted is a woman of integrity. She is a woman of morality. She lets a man know that she will be constant in her love. She lets a man know that she will not be moved, not by others' opinions nor their ideals. She will hold her man through right and wrong. As God holds all of us in His arms, as a mother holds a tempestuous child whose leaping about caused an injury to his knee, she can scold and correct, but her love is unfailing. If it is necessary to condemn his wrong, she does it without condemning him. She is a safe haven. She is the harbor where he docks his fears and finds shelter in the storm of life. She is the refuge to which he runs. If this trust exists, the marriage may be tested, but it will not die. It is built to stand against the winds of adversity. It is as strong as a rock, but to him it is as soft as a pillow. Tonight he will be home. For like any son of man, he has nowhere else to lay his head. Can he lay his head on you?

> And Jesus said unto him, Foxes have holes, and birds of the air have nests; but the Son of man hath not where to lay his head.   Luke 9:58

Many men feel as if they have no place to lay their heads. They continue looking— at work, on the sports field, in the bottom of a glass, in the arms of a painted woman whose name he doesn't even know. They are runners who cannot find the finish line. They are ships missing the port. They are rich and poor, black and white. They are wanderers, strangers traveling through life with a sad look on their faces. Woman is the ark God built to rescue man from the storm of life. She is the fortress to which he can escape from the mounting stress of day-to-day existence. She is the light in the night. She is the element of love and the instrument of passion. He cannot live without her, but where can he find her?

Chapter Eleven

Who Can Find a Virtuous Woman?

She does him good and not evil all the days of her life.   Prov. 31:12

A woman of virtue is rare indeed, but that is your challenge. Keep your heart focused and your gaze fixed. Be strong yet comforting, firm yet forgiving. Show your man that you are trustworthy. Guard his secrets and protect his heart. Praise him when he's worthy, and forgive him when he's not. Be his cheerleader, his confessor, his haven of love. Let him know you are committed to his good and will never do him evil. Be his lover, his soul mate, his friend. Be a woman of virtue!

One of the greatest gifts you can give a man is to be constant in your love. As I said earlier, men are often confused by women and what seems like erratic behavior. That confusion often leads to a heightened sense of vulnerability and insecurity. You see, anytime something is foreign, it makes people uncomfortable. Have you ever driven your car into an area that was unfamiliar? The drive seems long and tedious. Later, after you know your way around, it seems as if the trip is shorter and more comfortable. It is not that the road has changed, just your confidence about it. Suddenly you do not feel vulnerable because you know what to expect. When a woman changes, for whatever reason, a man feels vulnerable. He may still be driving, but he suddenly feels as if he is lost without a map. This is extremely troubling for a man, but he won't talk about it; he'll just shut down. Now, you women know a man won't ask for directions. He'll just drive around in circles, not knowing where he is going. The truth is he is afraid to admit that he's lost. Instead of asking for help, he gets angry, then he may start to drive recklessly, and before you know it he's driving off the road, and the relationship ends up in a ditch with a broken taillight and a dent in the fender.

A man is afraid of getting lost. He is not sure that the girl he marries will stay the same. It is fear that causes some men to avoid commitment. They feel as though they are committing to one woman who may suddenly click her heels and become someone else. This fear is intensified for a man who has a background laced with betrayals. I have counseled many men who have experienced a betrayal or a death; these men find it difficult to open up because they feel as though everyone they love leaves or betrays them. They resolve the conflict by locking up their emotions, and just when a woman needs them most, they are not there. A woman in need gets angry when her man isn't there for her. Then his sweet little pussycat may turn into a raging tigress. She is hurt because he is distant. He gets even more hurt because she is changing on him.

What a man wants is a contract, an iron-clad prenuptial agreement that promises the woman will not change. But no covenant will guarantee him that he will get the original woman in the original form with no alterations or addendums. It is not realistic to ask her not to change at all. Seasons change, weather changes, and men themselves change. The issue then is not a contract that guarantees no change; it is just that the man needs to feel her attitude toward him will not change. This is a very important issue for men. Will she change toward me? As she evolves into this thing called a mother, will she lose her exuberance, passion, appreciation, or attraction to me? These are the thoughts that haunt the hearts of many men who find it difficult to say "I do."

A man may be intimidated by a woman who is academically or economically superior to him. In many cases, it is not her larger income that challenges him; it is the fear that her superiority will change how she feels about him. He is afraid that her success will cause her to become condescending. But the wise woman knows that academic or financial success does not make her a better person. A marriage is a partnership in which one person complements the other, one's strength compensates for the weakness in the other, and vice versa. Both men and women should realize that it doesn't matter who has what individually; it is the sum of the parts that makes for a strong marriage.

Unfortunately, many men still need to

validate their masculinity through false images of virility. Money, sex, and power become the measuring sticks of strength. But this is not true. It is possible to have all three of these and still be a very weak man. Sadly, this truth has seldom been taught or learned in our society. Real strength cannot be counted in dollars or accredited at a university. Real strength is proven in a marriage by our resilience and commitment to the other in times of great challenge. In short, even if you have more degrees than a thermometer, more money than a bank vault, or are better looking than a Hawaiian sunset, if you lack the ability to be a partner in a storm, a soul mate in a time of desolation, you are nothing at all. Men and women need to learn that what they have accomplished pales when they have no one to behold its luster and stellar quality. What good is a career if there is no one with whom to share your accomplishments? What good is money if you have no one to help you enjoy it? Sooner or later we learn the perils of being alone. You don't have to be married to have someone in your life; you can share your life with parents or close friends. But woe to the one who has lived only for fame or fortune. In the end, fame can't hold you up when you stumble, and fortune can't keep you warm through the night.

My advice to a man who is married to an ambitious woman is simple: applaud her strength and fill her voids. She has them. We all do. There is room at the top for a man in the life of a successful woman. To the woman I say, make sure that the room in your life is well lit and easy for him to see. Do not spend your life trying to prove to someone whom you love that you do not need him, because he just may believe you and walk away. Show him the void, and he will fill it. Men were designed to fill your void. Seeing it is the greatest motivator the man can have. Madam, it is your void that motivates his strength. Showing him your space will heal the fear in him. Sir, if you see the light on, for God's sake, walk in. She is waiting for you.

A virtuous woman will never do her man harm. She is a wife. She is a treasure. The sister is awesome! She is the kind of woman whose support makes the difference. Weak? I don't think so! She is the combustion in an engine. She is the steam in an iron. She "does him good and not evil." She is a doer! This girl is no dreamer; she is no idle threat. She delivers like a pizza shop; she is at the door, on the mark, and prepared for the need. It is no wonder that she causes smiles to break out whenever she comes. She is passive, but aggressive. Not so passive that she is not able to take the initiative, yet she is not so aggressive that she leaves him no role to play. The lady is a doer, and she does him good! Do him, girl. He needs you. He needs you like the flowers need the rain. You are a part of his destiny, a component of his chemistry, the missing link. When he finds you, he knows he has found bone of his bone and flesh of his flesh.

She is his body. She is he. He should treat her with all the care with which he treats himself. She is not competition, so he should not feel threatened by her. He should feel complete in her. That is the goal, and together they can reach it. It is to this end that they pray. But do not stop in prayer. It is to this end that they touch. It is to this end that they come together in the light of the Lord to join in body, heart, and soul. It is awesome, and it takes a lifetime to complete, but what a wonderful journey!

Tragically, many men have not learned the art of encouraging their wives to be all that they can be. Rather, they choose to muzzle her creativity in an attempt to secure their position as the head. Sadly, they do not realize that if they are the head, she is the neck. And a weak neck is no help, even to a great head. It is to the man's advantage to encourage her to be all that she can be, because as she is, so is the man she loves. If she is insecure, it will affect him. It is to his advantage to have her healthy and whole. A man may like to keep her broken and dependent; it heightens his sense of control. But when both a man and a woman are healthy and whole, there is no need for control. They are partners, working together for the same goal.

A man doesn't have to fear a virtuous woman. There is no evil in her. No reason for him to be guarded. Her intentions are clearly seen. She has a commitment to assisting him, completing him, renewing him. He has to value her, as she is three times a lady: she is the mother he needed, the friend he never had, and the lover he dreamed about. This girl is too giving to be self-centered. It is not about her; it is all about him. Why should she worry about her needs anyway? That is what he is supposed to do. A virtuous woman is not for every man. Some couldn't handle love on her level. Send the boys to their rooms. This is a man's woman.

This girl is a ten. She is a queen like Esther. She is destined and reserved for a king.

> But with thee will I establish my covenant; and thou shalt come into the ark, thou, and thy sons, and thy wife, and thy sons' wives with thee. And of every living thing of all flesh, two of every sort shalt thou bring into the ark, to keep them alive with thee; they shall be male and female. Of fowls after their kind, and of cattle after their kind, of every creeping thing of the earth after his kind, two of every sort shall come unto thee, to keep them alive.
>
> Gen. 6:18–20

Woman, if you love like a princess, make sure that you do not yoke with a frog! All frogs do not turn into princes with a kiss. The principle of mating necessitates that each species mate after its kind. I realize that the emphasis here is on species, but I challenge you to go beyond biological likeness and identify psychological and spiritual likeness. For if you do not, you will find yourself attached to a frog, and you will spend all of your life trying to make him a prince. If you are a man, you will find yourself wanting a queen but you will find yourself attached to something that barks and chases cars down the street. How sad it is to find, years into the marriage, that you have chosen the wrong person. This is why bitterness erupts and marriages decompose. There is nothing wrong with marriage, but it works only when you marry your own kind. You might say that sounds like a racist remark, but what I am speaking of has nothing to do with race. It has something to do with taste. The ethnicity may be different, but if the mentality is different you are in for real trouble.

> Don't be teamed with those who do not love the Lord, for what do the people of God have in common with the people of sin? How can light live with darkness? And what harmony can there be between Christ and the devil? How can a Christian be a partner with one who doesn't believe? And what union can there be between God's temple and idols? For you are God's temple, the home of the living God, and God has said of you, "I will live in them and walk among them, and I will be their God and they shall be my people." That is why the Lord has said,

"Leave them; separate yourselves from them; don't touch their filthy things, and I will welcome you and be a Father to you, and you will be my sons and daughters."

II Cor. 6:14–18 (TLB)

Many people are unequally yoked. The Bible says that when Adam looked he could find no suitable help meet among all of the animals. That doesn't mean he couldn't find something that he could have forced. It just means that there was nothing there appropriate for him. There is more involved in selecting a mate than just finding someone who looks good or is simply willing. It is far deeper than that. Finding someone who has the same goals and lifestyle is crucial. It reminds me of the countless people who are waiting for a bone transplant. They desperately need to find someone who is suitable. Their problem isn't that no one cares or is willing to give it a try; it is just when the tests are done, they don't have a match. The body will not bond with what is unfamiliar, and neither should you.

As a woman, you would want someone who feels as if you have known him for years. You would want someone who reflects your needs and mirrors your life's goals. You would want someone who is comfortable and complements who you are and what you like to do. These qualities need to be inherent in the person. Never involve yourself with someone and think you are going to change them. Trust me, people seldom change, and if they do, it is only with God doing the changing.

As a man, you would want the woman of the Proverbs. This girl is a ten! In bed she is sensual; in prayer she is spiritual; in business she is shrewd. She is a resourceful, vibrant woman with ingenuity and self-esteem. This woman is a prize. She is comfortable in her femininity; she is not ashamed of her fragility for she knows that her silk covering is merely a mask for great inner strength and determination. She is not a manipulator; she is too strong in her own right to need to live the desperate life of a deceitful woman. Her only concern is finding the right man, the one she can assist in fulfilling their destiny. This is not everybody's woman. She is as radiant as a star. She will not stoop to looking for love. She stands out in the night. Love will find her. When it does, it will rock the planet. She is a woman of excellence.

Let Him Come Home

Beneath the roar of the masculine voice there is a whimpering lamb. "Do me good!" he cries. "Love me good, hold me good, touch me good, and speak comfortably to me. For you are my only friend, my confidant, my only place of rest. It is you that I want to impress. Do not make it so hard that I feel it is impossible to win a compliment in my own home." Ask any woman who has ever loved a great man, and she will tell you that she has seen a little boy peeking out of the window of his soul. Sometimes the little boy trembles and cries to be held, but the man that envelops him will not allow it. If a woman's frame is wrapped in soft skin and less muscle mass, that doesn't mean she doesn't have a will of iron. But what she needs to know is that her husband is the opposite. He is wrapped in hard muscles, but beneath this rugged exterior are the ingredients that teddy bears are made of. He needs her to respect the package that he comes in but still touch the contents that it hides from her view.

When love is in sync, he will feel as though she is the haven to which he must run. When life has beaten him up, he should be so sure she is on his side that his thoughts immediately run toward home like a child who fell and scraped his knee. He knows that home is the place of comfort. He is assured that there he will be done good and not evil. No one runs toward a nagging voice. No one would run toward a room filled with continual complaints. If you have a problem, voice it, but do not allow your presence to become associated with discomfort. You have the power to become associated in his mind with a place of good and not evil. You can become a clinician of affection and a Florence Nightingale to the damaged soldier. The sound of your voice will either draw him or drive him away. A weary soldier never wants to come home to fight. He has fought his way to you.

When the voice at home is screaming in his ear, why should he bother going home? When he walks through the door and is assaulted by complaints, he may be tempted to walk right back out. The roof may be leaking, the baby may have cried all day, and the rent may be due, but if that's all he has to look forward to at home, he may have second thoughts about going there. Now, I'm not saying that you shouldn't share your challenges with your man, but when he comes home at night, give him a kiss on the cheek, let him sit in a chair, and tell him how glad you are to see him. If he doesn't feel welcomed at home, he may find another place to hang his hat. This is when the "other woman" becomes so enticing. Of course, sometimes even when home is a haven, a man may be tempted to stray. Marriage isn't always easy. It is grounded in reality where roofs leak, babies cry, and bills need to be paid. An illicit affair pulls with the promise of excitement and passion, and sometimes this pull is hard for a man to resist.

There are times in a man's life when this pull is harder. Like the changing tides of the sea, there are times in a man's life when the waves are stronger. Tragically, most men are not educated about the changes they will face, so when they come they are unprepared, embarrassed, and they withdraw. Whom can he talk to about hair loss, his strength loss, and other changes that seem to threaten his masculinity? Whom can he tell that he's tired, depressed, and frightened that he is no longer the man he used to be? Many marriages survive the turbulence of youth only to be shipwrecked after the children are grown. What is this rock that cracks the foundation of marriages we once admired? In many cases, it is the challenged masculine heart that has no one to talk to and dies in silent screams of frustration and fear. Men are not like women. Women share with each other what it is like for them at various stages. Men have some secret code of silence. This secret code has damned the destiny of many men who could have been salvaged.

What sailor would want to sail without a forecast of the pending changes in weather? Yet most men sail the sea of life ignorant of any changes to their bodies, their needs, and attitudes. My sister, your mate may sail into a storm and say nothing at all. It is not always his attempt at deceit that holds his tongue. Many times it is his fear and stress. If he only knew that you would do him good. I know you would, but does he? Tell him! He may need to hear it. Better yet, he may need to see it. Do not be discouraged if he doesn't open up immediately. He will be afraid. Even talkative men are quite silent about things that really bother them.

When he does swallow his fear and risk his image to open up to you, when he tells you that he is troubled, depressed, or feels a loss of purpose, virility, or excitement, when he tells you that the stress at work has robbed him of the passion he once had, just listen. Resist the urge to go on a tangent about those people on that job and how you always said they were just using him anyway. It is not important that you are right. Never say "I told you so." Your husband is trying to scream out for help in a storm. This is not a game; put away your scoreboard and just be his friend. Do not interrupt. What good is it to win the score if you lose this precious moment of communication and throw him into another year of sullen silence? Let him talk to you, and listen! He may be terrified that he is mortal, and the loss of his teeth and the balding of his head may make him feel old. He may have a waning passion level, or he may have begun to develop ailments and afflictions. He may need to tell you that the reason he has started to flirt is that he feels unattractive and elderly, and he finds himself wondering if anyone finds him attractive. He may need reassurance and affirmation. Give him the chance to tell you what he needs, then just give it to him.

These are often the times in your relationship when Satan would set you up to be so busy that you are distracted. It is possible not to be there for someone you love.

Not because you do not care, but because you are spread so thin in other areas. After all, what about the kids? This is about the time they are dating or in college. You have a career or your own involvements as well. Besides, when you were trying to be there before, he was distracted, so you adjusted and now have other things that occupy your time. And just when you've gotten used to his not being there, he changes his tune. The truth of the matter is that "Mr. No Time for Intimacy" has finally woken up, and he needs something you have been trying to tell him about for years. He needs affection and intimacy—not just sex, but this is so foreign to him he doesn't even know how to ask for it. And by the time he does, if you are not careful, you may be unable to give it to him. Perhaps you have endured some pains in your relationship that have left you wounded and hurt, guarded and aloof. Is there any forgiveness in you? If you miss this wonderful opportunity to rekindle what should become a deeper, richer, more balanced love than any you have ever experienced, you will continue to limp in pain and he . . . well, he will just shy away! He should fight for intimacy, but he won't. He is undereducated about the issue and overly egotistical regarding the problem. He will cry when you are not looking. He will whimper in the middle of the night. But in the light of morning, he will just shy away.

> If I take the wings of the morning, and dwell in the uttermost parts of the sea . . .   Ps. 139:9

You may wonder what the psalm means by "wings of the morning." It refers to the wings of possibility. The wings of new beginnings and second chances. The fresh wings that spread in the rested heart of someone who has refreshed himself in the night. Many fail to appreciate the manifold splendor of a new day. Morning is a victory to the one who travailed all night long. For the ailing, diseased patient, it is a triumph to see another day. To the aspiring businessperson, it is a fresh chance to achieve. To the artist, it is a chance to catch the winking sunrise that erupts across the plains. The wings of the morning are to be taken. They are to be seized and enjoyed. Many have not flown because they have not taken the wings of the morning. But they are spread before you. Do not miss them another day. You always have the option at the end of a perilous day to arise fresh and ascend into the future, spiraling in the wind and riding above the storm on the wings of the morning. Take the wings of the morning, resurrect your relationship, and heal yourself. Take the wings and lift yourself up to a place of excellence.

With every sunrise, recognize the light of God shining down on you. Know that He has watched over you through the night. He cares for you and baptizes you in the new day. The morning is a time of healing. It is a new day, a second chance, a fresh start. No wonder the proverb challenges the woman of excellence to take full advantage of the morning.

Part Three

Her Lord

Chapter Twelve

Embracing Her Lord

There is no relationship the lady can experience that is any more fulfilling than the relationship that exists between her and her Lord. It is being held in His everlasting arms that brings about healing from the damages that she has incurred in her pursuit of every other relationship. In His arms, she finds restoration. There will be times when she feels like a little girl, and in His presence she will climb into the lap of a loving Father whose sound wisdom, counsel, and consistent love will insulate her from the adversary whom she must fight. Her Father becomes her protector. He protects her by His Spirit. He counsels her by His Word. He forgives her through His blood, and she is safe in His arms.

He is the solace that heals the feminine soul and renews her mind. He is the missing ingredient that adds validity to every other pursuit of her life. If she gains everything and fails to know Him, she has nothing at all. His love for her is so pure that she will find no other like it. It is not predicated upon her performance or her appearance or her intellectual capacity. He has loved her before she was formed in the womb of her mother. His love is holy. It becomes the foundation that her character is built upon. The woman who knows the love of God is not desperate for the love of men because in His arms she has already found that for which her soul thirsts. Now, this is not to say that having Christ will fulfill every void that she has as a woman. But her satisfaction in His presence is so complete that it removes her far away from the desperate need for affection and affirmation that leads other women to grope and grasp blindly in the night. She can run to Him in every crisis and know that He will not fail her, He will not desert her, He will not leave her, and He will not change.

Strangely, women seem to possess some

special ability to touch the heart of God. It is so powerful that Jeremiah, the weeping prophet who was known to be a man of great compassion, still found himself needing the intercessory power of women to touch the heart of God. He said, "Send for the women of mourning and let them take up a wailing" (Jer 9:17). It's as if he knows that God's ears are open to the cry of distressed women. It is not that God favors women over men, but the Lord looks out for His daughters and takes care of their needs. Jesus promises, "If you believe on me as the scripture has said, then out of your belly shall flow rivers of living water" (John 7:38). I then challenge you, in accordance to His Word, to believe in Him. You have believed in others and have been disappointed. You have believed in others and have been rejected. But this is a promise from a man who cannot lie. The challenge is for the woman to believe in Him. If you will, there will be no drought in your heart, no dryness in your spirit, and no emptiness in your life, for God will quench your thirst with living water.

There is no feeling as demanding as the thirst for water. Our bodies cannot do without water. Thirst is an incessant craving from the innermost parts of our being that will find fulfillment only as we lift to our mouths the cooling flow of refreshing water and drink deeply of it. It is this renewing, resuscitating feeling that God has promised the woman who believes in Him. Now, there are many women who have tried to quench their thirst in entrepreneurial pursuits, working feverishly to attain a position of power and financial gain. There are many women whose beauty and curvaceous bodies have allowed them to choose any man whom they would like. They have jumped from bed to bed and from arm to arm trying to find satisfaction in sexual entanglements. There are even those ladies who are so romantically inclined that, although they fled from the temptations of promiscuity, they were vulnerable to any sign of affection shown to them from a male suitor. But there is something that every wise woman must understand. There is no human relationship that can quench the thirst of the soul like the touch of God.

If you have been searching all of your life for something that seems to evade you, if you have diligently pursued success and all of its many trappings and still there is an aching inside that reminds you something is missing, I would like to recommend the only thirst quencher that can satisfy the longing of the human soul. His name is Jesus. His arms are stretched wide. His voice is calm. His wisdom is stable. His counsel is sure. And He will hold you through the night. It is time for you to open yourself to knowing Him in a deeper way than you have ever known Him before. He is more than a weekly visitation to a stone building that we call a church. He is more than the historical perspective we find in the leather-bound book we call a Bible. He is more than a morsel of bread and a small cup of wine we call communion. He is the epitome of life. He is the central force from which all things emerge. "By him all things consist" (Col. 1:17).

Jesus is the secret weapon of the woman who is armed for the times. She carries him everywhere she goes. Whether she walks with an attaché case and dresses in a business suit or she stays at home warming nursing bottles, He is her secret weapon. Without Him, she will always be vulnerable. Without Him, she will never be sure of anything, sure of anyone, or sure of herself. He is the foundation from which she builds.

You may ask, "How can I embrace a God I cannot see? What comfort will I derive from speaking to a God I cannot hear?

What fulfillment can be gained from intimacy with a God I cannot touch?" I'm glad you asked. God is not a man. You do not approach Him with your flesh. He is in your heart. It is in the very depths of your spirit that you can touch Him. And if you listen with your inner ear, you can hear Him speak to you. When life is at its worst, He speaks the loudest. You can embrace Him through praise. In order to praise Him, you must believe in Him. In order to raise your hands and smile at a God who cannot be seen, you must be a woman of faith, a woman who believes. In order to wake up in the morning and place your feet on the floor and lift your head toward heaven and thank Him for another day, you must be a woman who is intuitive enough to sense that you did not wake up by yourself. It is this kind of believing that releases the fountain of living water. It is believing Him to have the compassion to navigate you through the clutter and chaos of life. It is believing that when seemingly senseless tragedy strikes, He will not allow you to fall. This level of faith may make some sneer and laugh, but it is the kind of faith that releases the water a woman needs to survive. If a woman draws her water from Him, then she will not feel so parched in the presence of people. She will not walk through life with vulnerable eyes and a questioning expression on her face. She will wake up singing in the morning, fulfilled in the day, and complete in the night because she has found Him whom her soul loveth.

The Doctor Is In

And a certain woman, which had an issue of blood twelve years, And had suffered many things of many physicians, and had spent all that she had, and was nothing bettered, but rather grew worse, When she had heard of Jesus, came in the press behind, and touched his garment. For she said, If I may touch but his clothes, I shall be whole. And straightway the fountain of her blood was dried up; and she felt in her body that she was healed of that plague.   Mark 5:25–29

Like the famous woman with the issue of blood, each woman, in her own way, gropes to touch the hem of God's garment. It is a long, dusty journey. It is a journey that is cluttered with life's experiences and many, many false physicians. You will notice that the woman with the issue of blood had been treated by many physicians before she came to Christ. In some ways, I believe her pain was multiplied by the many attempts that man had made to fix a problem that only God can cure. It is the mistake of many to look to a man to do what only God can do. Ultimately, only God has the capacity to put an end to suffering. Only He has the ability to end the searching of the feminine heart whose problems have been exaggerated by the aching disappointment that comes from being treated by those who do not have the cure for the pain. This kind of disappointment is always going to occur when the woman looks to man to do what only God can do. Enjoy your husband and his love, but please know that there is some healing that is far beyond the eros kind of love. It will take the *agape* love—the God kind of love. It heals with one touch what man cannot do in many touches. This is not meant to minimize the marital relationship. It is meant to put it in perspective, so disappointment and bitterness do not evolve from the heart of a woman who has been made to believe that a man can do what only God's grace can do.

We have talked about the lady and we have talked about her lover, but there is nothing more important than talking about her Lord. A woman needs to heal herself. She needs to find and maintain a relationship with a husband that will allow her to fulfill her potential. But ultimately, she will yearn for fulfillment in an area that is far deeper than human hands can reach. Whether or not she knows how to ask for it or where to find it, she is ultimately seeking the touch of her Lord. Many women need the hand of the Lord in their lives, but because they do not understand what exactly is lacking in their lives, they chase after things like a career, education, and affluence. None of these things are dangerous in and of themselves, but when they become a substitute for God, a person will be left terribly dissatisfied. After years of building a career and chasing success, they will find that without God all things are hollow and worthless. I call these things the imitations of life. As all imitations, they have certain qualities that would deceive the less discerning eye, but under closer scrutiny, the connoisseur can easily detect that the imitation is in no way worthy to be compared to the original. What is the original? you ask. The original is the thing that Eve first had in the garden. It is fellowship with the Lord. If the woman has this kind of fellowship to minister to her spirit, if she has creative thoughts to massage her mind, and a companion to touch her flesh, then she has everything. No matter how wealthy or successful she is, if she does not have Christ, she is as poor as the Laocedonian church. It is this church that Revelation 3 declares had a reputation for being wealthy but in truth was wretched, naked, and blind.

Years of emptiness and despair create a hollowness within a woman that causes the heart to ache and eyes to lose their luster. Suddenly she has an inner blemish that makeup will not cover and jewelry will not hide. It is the innate awareness that somewhere within her spirit there is the most engulfing poverty she has ever known. How foolish it is to think that this poverty can be healed by human hands. This is the kind of emptiness that only the Lord can eradicate. I challenge you to allow Him to touch you and make you whole.

Oh, I know you have been to many physicians, and their lofty promises and frail pharmaceuticals have failed to erase your past and ease your turmoil. Those promises haunt your mind, torment your spirit, and frustrate

250

your flesh. Perhaps God allows us to pursue the false physicians long enough, so when we encounter Him we appreciate Him all the more. Perhaps He allows the physicians to practice their worthless medicine so that when we do touch something real we can easily identify it as the cure for our ailment. Whatever the reason, most women have encountered the touch of a worthless physician. They have ridden a roller coaster of false expectations only to have another relationship crumble, another promise broken, and another hope destroyed. But do not be embittered by this. Just run as fast as you can— walk if you must, in fact crawl if necessary—to the Word of God. There are some times when a lady cannot heal herself; there are times when her lover cannot stitch the jagged edges of her broken heart. Then she must reach out to her Lord. It was this Lord that the woman with the issue of blood touched at a moment of crisis in her life, and immediately she knew within herself that she was made whole. There is nothing as comforting as knowing that you are whole. Neither success nor fame can bring the peaceful smile and calmness of spirit that rises within someone who has recognized that they are not fractional anymore but they are whole and complete. For when a woman is whole, she can enter into a relationship without desperation; she does not need anyone to complete her. She has become complete by the touch of the Lord Himself.

A whole woman will always attract a whole man. And when they touch, they will fuse to create a whole marriage. Ultimately, when the time is right, they will produce whole children who will benefit from nursing at the breast of a woman who is not plagued with a desperate need for self-gratification. This is the result of a God-centered life. This woman is a virtuous woman. She is filled with virtue. You will notice that when Jesus healed the woman with the issue of blood He knew she had been healed because He felt the virtue leave His body. It is the virtue that left Him and entered into her body that made her whole. Through a touch from God, she became a virtuous woman. You ask, "How can I get this virtue?" It is not in a career. It is not in success. It is not in fine clothes, fancy cars, or expensive jewelry. The virtue comes only when a broken woman crawls the cobblestone streets of Jerusalem on bloody knees and her trembling hand extends to touch the hem of a Lord whose presence can eradicate the pain in her life.

That touch is so awesome that it inspires her to become a virtuous woman. All those that come near her will know that there is some distinction about her—whether she is in the executive office turning around in the swivel chair, or she has entered the office only to clean it for some executive who employs her. It does not matter, because she is filled with virtue. There is a glimmer in her eyes that makes cosmetics unnecessary. There is a peace in her mind that has alleviated any need for narcotics. She sleeps at night. She rises refreshed. She faces each day with courage because her strength is not coming from the external; it is embedded in the internal. Because she has touched her Lord, she is complete and totally whole. When the woman touches her Lord, He changes her forever. Her soul escapes like a bird from the snare of the fowler. Her wings spread in the morning. She sails on the wind, and she flies into the brightness of the morning sun. He is the object of her adoration and the focal point of her vision. He becomes the reality of every abstract idea she has ever struggled to articulate to others who did not understand.

Now, you must understand that all of us yearn to have and deeply enjoy human relationships. But only the wisest of us will ever come truly to understand that the level of fulfillment we need cannot come from another person. The reason our human relationships shred into pieces and crumble to the floor is that we have the audacity to seek in men what can only come from God. We will always be disappointed when we seek God in man and desire men to be our heroes. I fear that we have read too many novels suggesting a chivalry that does not exist. Like the tarnished face of silver, we soon recognize that what glitters and gleams in the noonday sun will eventually dull when it is exposed to the elements. So it is with all men—sooner or later we will discover that there are tarnished places, and none of us, neither male nor female, shines as brightly as we need to shine.

Where are the heroes? you ask. Where are the noblemen? Where are all the perfect, euphoric relationships we saw on TV? I must tell you that they were just figments of our imagination, caricatures displayed on the screen for our entertainment. Though we work feverishly to duplicate what we saw, we must realize that the end result is guaranteed for the couple on television because a script controls their lives. But what can we do when there is no script to control the events that happen from day to day? The truth of the matter is there is nothing you can do. There will be no perfect companions. There will be no love without disappointment. But the disappointment is minimized when we expect certain things only from God. If we seek a savior, His name must be Jesus. If we seek a messiah, it must be the Christ. To ask anyone other than Him to rise to such an expectation is to ask a clay pot to be gold. It is to ask water to be wine. It is to ask dirt to be diamonds. It cannot be. So, my dear sister, if you are going to touch the divine and feel the power of God, you will only do that when you reach beyond human flesh and aspire to know the Creator in all of His many facets and forms. Oh yes, you will see traces of Him in men, in children, and even in yourself. But these mere traces will never be enough to support the weight of everything you ever experienced. These traces of God will lack the virtues that are needed to heal the wretchedness of your past and dismiss the ghosts that haunt the secret chambers of your memory and imagination. This is a job for God and God alone. The prophet said, "Seek the Lord while he may be found, call upon Him while He is near" (Isa. 55:6). He has spoken well. It is time to seek the Lord, not His children, not His gift, but His person and that alone. For when we seek Him, then it is His good pleasure to give to each of us the benefits that are derived only from our relationship with Him.

It is amazing to me that a God so holy could reach so low and touch a broken world. It reminds me of the moment in the Scriptures when they brought before Jesus a woman who was caught in the act of adultery. They had dragged her battered body roughly down the streets of Jerusalem into the presence of the Rabbi, the Master, the Teacher Himself. Her nude body was bruised at the hands of self-righteous men who thought themselves judges of her decadence. They pushed and shoved her while she wailed in shame and despair and tried to cover herself. They accused her and demeaned her and finally brought her before Jesus. They had planned to stone her. They had planned to mock her shame and debauchery, and to put on public display her private weakness. To their amazement, Jesus did not join them in the lynching of this woman. Instead He seemed distracted from the whole event. The Scripture says He stooped down and took His finger and began to write in the dirt. It is that stooping action that fascinates my mind. That someone so high could stoop so low. I do not pretend to know why He wrote. I am not sure it is important what He wrote. What's far more important for me to know is that God can stoop to my level and write in my life. It is important for me to articulate to you that there are those of us whose flaws and spotted pasts would cause us to be stoned and tackled, and yet somehow His infinite grace and mercy embrace us. In the face of our greatest accusers, he has the ability to look beyond our faults and see our needs.

Who would not love a God like this? Who would not wash His feet with tears? Who would not raise her hands in His presence? Or kiss His nail-scarred hands, when these are the hands that reach out to heal the broken areas in her life? A woman needs to know that there is a God who can know her darkest, deepest secrets and still have compassion for her. What woman would not tremble in the presence of a God who would assume the task of defending her and stand between her and her assailants? What woman would not appreciate a God who becomes an attorney, assumes her case, requires no fee, and wins her the victory? What woman would not be awed to know that there is a

God who can be convinced of her guilt and yet insist on her forgiveness? This is the epitome of love: to know that we are all naked before Him and yet somehow He, by His grace, stoops down and touches the dirty places in our lives.

It is recognizing this kind of mercy and grace that causes the woman of the twenty-first century to fall in love with the God who is called the "Ancient of Days." He is older than time itself, and yet He is more relevant than this morning's paper. He is before when or where; He is before this or that. And yet He is the God who is never referred to in the past tense. He is not the God that was; He is the God that is. He is the God that is called I Am. I Am what? you ask. He is whatever you need Him to be, whenever you need Him to be. I am sorry, and I apologize on behalf of all the men of the world because none of us can be whatever you want us to be whenever you want us to be. No one can be this but God. He is the absolute of which we are just a shadow. He is the reality of which we are just a substitute. We can hold you through the night, but He can hold you through the ages. So when our arms grow weak and weary, we can recommend a God who neither sleeps nor slumbers.

He can stop the stones that should have been hurled at you. One word from Him gives you the second chance you need to succeed. Your husband may be the lover of your body, but He is the lover of your soul. Your husband may kiss your lips, but He can kiss the tears from your eyes, the pain from your memories, the clouds from your skies. He is the great lover. He paid the price to bear the name. He shed the blood that became the evidence, and became the judge of this world to throw your case out of court. Because of Him, you are free.

The Ultimate Love Affair

Now, with the skill of a surgeon, I must take these next words and carefully make an incision with the scalpel of truth. I pray that I might be endowed by God with the ability to make the necessary distinction between having a relationship with the institution of the church and knowing the Christ to which the church worships. I certainly do not want to imply that uniting with a place of worship is not Biblical. It certainly is Biblical. It is also appropriate. To worship with other believers magnifies the intensity of the personal experience that we have shared with an invisible God. The invisible God seems almost to manifest in the presence of communal worship. When we collectively celebrate our faith, we are intensified through our unified praise and worship.

Yet I must caution you that there are many women who have fled the chaos of the clubs, the decadence of broken relationships, and have run into the sanctuary of the church only to be riddled again by pain. That is not to suggest that there is a flaw in the church. The church is designed to be a place of worship and that is all. We must understand that the institution of the church is not the Savior. It is the Christ of the church that saves, and I am afraid—no, I am terrified— by the many, many people who seek refuge in the church without discovering the Christ behind the church. Without Christ, the church is just one more worthless physician.

These precious women join the institution of the church as if it were merely a sorority, a women's club, a lodge, a place for social gathering and the exhibition of gifts, skills, and social class. They may even worship with great demonstration and express adoration with passion. Yet secretly, when they are taken off the stage and away from the audience of other believers, they have no personal experience with the Lord. I must caution you—no, I must challenge you—to reach through the veil of the church and touch in its very womb the Christ child Himself. For until you touch Him, you will never really be made whole. You will be surprised how many women come to church week after week, service after service, and fail to become impregnated with the potent seed of the Word of God.

We must understand that Christ is the object of our pursuit, and His church is just one of the ways that we access Him. I realize that one does not need to attend a church to encounter Christ. He will appear in your room or in your car. He can even bring His presence to you now as you contemplate His Word. But having experienced Him, you will ultimately find yourself yearning to be surrounded by other believers who understand the magnitude of your experience. Yes, congregational worship is important and essential, but the gathering of people without the presence of Christ is a futile exchange of human interests, religious rhetoric, and jargon that does not bring life.

You must be a cunning woman. A cunning woman is a woman who is intelligent and discerning enough to know what it is she needs and who possesses the ability to accomplish the goal she has determined. The goal is to have an intimate, personal relationship with God. He then becomes the underground water that replenishes the dry soil and prepares your ground for the abundant harvest of blessing that is promised through His Word. You must pursue him with passion. You must pursue him with intensity. I cannot explain it, but there seems to be some depth of worship that the feminine heart has a tendency to reach but only few men will ever encounter. It seems that women somehow understand how to lose themselves in the presence of God in a unique and powerful way. Once a woman understands that Christ is her goal, she seems able to focus on Him, allure Him, and entertain Him with a level of praise that is so engrossing that she is healed by His touch and fulfilled by His Word. I have seen women who were so impacted by His invisible presence that they were able to walk away from the presence of others who were far more tangible, but far less effective. In short, I have seen many sisters walk away from a man they could see toward a God they could not see and find in His presence the peace that evaded them all of their lives.

These women praise the Lord with a romanticism that is so engrossing. They write Him poetry and sing Him songs. They dance in His presence. They raise their hands toward Him in the middle of the night. They walk through the house exchanging thoughts and pleasantries. They seem almost like little girls sitting in the lap of an aged father whose touch is so loving. These women arise from the altar of praise and walk the streets of life with an inner confidence and an inner knowing that cause them to have a smile for which no man is responsible. These are the daughters of Sarah.

In order to be Sarah's daughter you must be a woman whose relationship with God is so intense that when she is faced with challenges she refuses to be intimidated or overwhelmed. In fact, she resists the temptation to be traumatized by the crises of life. She chooses to walk in the full assurance that the presence of God is there to walk beside her. She knows God as an ultimate husband. She has seen Him open doors for her. She has seen Him provide for her every need. His word has counseled her about tomorrow's plight, and because of Him she is whole. She is Sarah's daughter. She refuses to be struck with amazement or filled with bewilderment.

She breathes in the good of life and exhales the bad of life. And the cycle continues without asphyxiation because she has learned that all these things are but a process, a process that will lead her closer to the presence of God.

The woman who has found Christ to be the lover of her soul is rich indeed. This is a love affair that time will not eradicate. This is the ongoing internal touching of spirits. The woman who has found Christ dances to the beat of another drummer. She seems to hear things that other women do not hear. She has a sense of fulfillment that often intimidates many men. She lies in the bed at night alone but not lonely. She knows that she has nestled herself down into the cradle of His love and that she has wrapped herself up in His divine favor. She will be strong and not weak. She will live and not die. She will fight and not faint. Because He is she will be also.

Occasionally, when life sends perils or distresses, you will see this woman slip away from the crowd to be alone. Alone? No, not really. She yearns to slip away from the clamoring sound of men and women whose words do not fulfill her inner needs. She yearns to be with Him. Like a young lover slipping away at night, she finds herself disengaging from the conversations of frivolous people to allow herself undistracted attention in the presence of her Lord. He is the wind beneath her wings. When He breathes upon her, she soars in the wind of His breath. He fuels her. He invigorates her. He motivates her. When she faces obstacles, He whispers encouragement in her ears. He is the lover of her soul. The hymnist said it more eloquently than I could ever declare: "Jesus lover of my soul, let me through thy bosom fly." It is by resting on His bosom that we are able to lay our weary heads of adversity upon the Breasted One, to be able to climb into His everlasting arms and know that we are kept by the grace of a God whose sovereign mercy has made a complete decision about us, and we are forever, irrevocably, accepted by the Beloved.

Oh, what a feeling it is to finally find someone whose love is not predicated upon our performance. What a peace it is for all of us, male or female, to lay down the frivolous pursuits of impressions and to be free to climb unashamedly into the presence of a God whose heart is filled with passion for us. How wonderful to know that His every thought is only for our good. Oh, yes, He is the lover of our souls. How much more is He attracted to the woman who responds to His touch with her praise. She is the woman whose manners mandate that she always say, "Thank you." She is far too gracious to be stabilized by His power and then rob Him of His glory by taking credit for herself. She knows that behind every line of her success and every page of her accomplishments, He is the paper that her commendations are written on. He is the center and the focal point of her life. And if you look closely, you will see her reach out to Him.

As I close this thought and move on to another, I challenge you to respond to Him though you cannot see Him. He is not far from you. He is so close to you, waiting just to hold you, waiting just to bless you. He is the lover of your soul. Reach out to Him, not just to His church. Not just to His gift. Not just to the day He has so graciously given you. Reach out to Him. Allow Him to kiss the tears from your face. Allow Him to brush back your hair, hold you in His arms, and rock you in His own divine purpose. You are too authentic to be duplicated. You are far too precious to be misappropriated. He has sent his angels to watch over you. They are guarding you, and because He is so in love with you, no weapon formed against you shall be able to prosper. If ever there were someone worth touching, if ever there were someone worthy of your attention, if ever there were someone who had the right to expect your adoration, it would be He. He is the lover of your soul. He is the lover of your past, present, and future. Hear me, my dear lady, He is your Lord.

Chapter Thirteen

Lord of Her Past

That Christ may dwell in your hearts by faith; that ye, being rooted and grounded in love, May be able to comprehend with all saints what is the breadth, and length, and depth, and height; And to know the love of Christ, which passeth knowledge, that ye might be filled with all the fullness of God.   Eph. 3:17–19

I would like to take this opportunity to introduce you to an aspect of the Lord you might seldom hear heralded across the pulpit of our country. Although many of God's "pulpiteers" praise the wondrous love of God, very few ever attempt to describe it. For how could we describe that which defies reason? To what can we compare the love of God? You must understand that when it comes to passion, he is incomparable. There is no one anywhere on the planet whose intensity can compare to the magnitude of God Himself. His passion is so overwhelming that the most moving saga or touching ballad does not portray it sufficiently. He is more rhythmic than poetry, more ardent than ballads of love. His love is bluer than the sea, brighter than the sun, and stronger than the wind that brushes through the trees. His love has seldom been taught, understood, or sadly enough, received. I can only but attempt to describe what the Bible declares to be "the love of Christ which passeth knowledge."

The astronaut, who has ascended beyond the gravitational pull of the earth, left behind our planet, traveled through our galaxy, and observed with close scrutiny the stars and planets from his lofty height, has not been able to go beyond the height of the love of God. And the archaeologist, who has dug to great depths into the dark soil and entered into the layers beneath the earth's surface so deep that he can feel the warmth of the center of the earth itself, has not plummeted to a depth so low that the love of God cannot reach. From north to south, from east to west, the breadth of God's love defies every method of measurement. It is what the Bible declares to be past knowledge. That phrase implies that we cannot totally know the love of God.

While we cannot know it, we can with wondrous humility aspire to know it. We can endeavor to perceive it. We can strain to see it. We can leap to reach it, though we understand before our futile attempt begins that at the apex of our endeavor we will fail to grasp the magnitude and the awesomeness of the love of a God whose grace defies the finite mind. All I can say is that when God Himself prepares to describe the crucifixion in the first chapter of the Book of Acts He describes it as "his passion." When I think of the cross, I think of the agony, the shame, the beating of his flesh, the bruising of his face, the plucking of his beard, the nailing of his soft youthful skin to a rugged tree. When I think of the cross, it is the most grotesque picture of murder ever painted on the face of time. It was so awful that the sun was ashamed; the ground became so uncomfortable that it began to tremble. The cross. The place of agony. The place where love was placed on trial and sentenced to death. It was the place where the great lover had to prove how much he "so loved the world."

It was after He was risen from the dead that He looks back on His night of horror, and He is filled with neither regret nor hostility, anger nor revenge. He refers to it as passion. Suddenly, I recognize that He is far more passionate than anything or anyone we will ever encounter. For if He can look at His own pain and refer to it as "passion," then I must recognize that God loves us in a way so far beyond anything we can refer to as love. For who else but God can decide to write us a love letter with his own flesh, use His hand for paper, release His blood for ink, and declare His passion in the most vibrant shade of red? Oh yes, what a lover He is!

May I take this opportunity to illustrate Him through the life of the prophet Hosea? It was to this young man, this young prophet, that He spoke a word. I want to take the details of this powerful Bible story and dramatize them, so through the details you might better grasp the impact of the original text. The reason that God directs this young man's life is to dramatically depict the magnitude of His great love. He needed someone to understand the level of His passion, so He spoke to this nice, neat, clean, upright young prophet who had kept himself unspotted from the world and reserved himself for a young maiden. This young man, who had no doubt fantasized with visions of grandeur some fair maiden who would be appropriated to him for matrimony, must have been astonished when he received from God the directive to choose his bride. God did not send him to the temple to select from the virgins an appropriate companion. Neither did he send him among the fine princesses who had been trained and manicured for a person of his stature. Instead, He told the young prophet to go down into the worst neighborhood in the city and choose a wife whose past is so smudged and blotted with degrading sins that no one would ever want her. What a shock it must have been to this young prophet that God would ask him to marry a whore. That's what she was. She was what our mothers would have called a slut. She was a street woman. She was a woman who had been passed around from man to man, bed to bed. She had been mauled like fruit at a fruit stand. She had been scarred and bruised. Many men had passed long hours fondling her and entertaining themselves with her. She had been the object of their lust. She was a woman of the night. She was a harlot, and yet God had selected her to be his wife.

On first glimpse, we would think that the story was an example of complete and total obedience, as if it were a matter of obeying God even when one felt like disobeying him. But that is not the crux of the story. It would have been amazing enough to see this prophet was so submitted that he would obey God even when God's Word would bring shame and criticism. But the real issue, the one that seems difficult to explain, is that when Hosea saw this woman he actually loved her. I am sure he expected to be dragged into this marriage full of anxiety and frustration, but that was not the case. You see, God created within him a passion for this unlovable person. That is what God often does—love the unlovable.

How could it be possible that a young man who is so clean could love a girl so filthy? Her name was Gomer. The name Gomer means "complete," but she was anything but complete. At least she wasn't when he met her, but that is not to say that she wasn't before all had been said and done. You see, his name is Hosea, which means "deliverance." And whenever deliverance is at work, you will always end up complete.

When Hosea saw Gomer, he just loved her. Whom could he tell that he had fallen in love with a whore? Who would believe it? How ridiculous! Everybody knows that no man falls in love with a whore. She would have been something to be toyed with like a kitten plays with yarn: touched, used, and then walked away from. But no, when he saw her, he absolutely loved her. You see, "deliverance" saw her "complete." He saw her potentials, and he saw her future. He assumed the task of untangling her from her past so that she could be complete in her future. That is the task that all wounded souls must assume. It is the task of moving beyond the tragedies of life into the potentials of our future.

Now close your eyes a moment and imagine Hosea standing on one street corner looking at Gomer standing on the other. There his fiancée stands, parading herself like a wholesaler selling her wares. Two bits, four bits, six bits, a dollar. She is in the discount section of degradation. She stands there like a side of beef with a price tag on every part of her body. She is someone everyone else lusted for and yet when Hosea looked at her, his heart flipped in passion. Songs burst forth in his spirit. He did not see her as a whore; he saw her as a wife. He saw her as the mother of his children. He saw her as a precious gem. He fell in love with her. They seemed an odd match. They were not equally yoked. They were not comparable people. They had not attended the same university. But if there is one thing all of us know, it is that sometimes love is not rational. It can even be ridiculous to those who watch from the sidelines.

But the Bible says Hosea's love affair is a mere depiction of how God felt when He loved His people. To think that He would love people like us! Have you ever done anything that was so horrendous you lost respect for yourself? Do you have hidden in your closet, behind your coats and dresses, a secret skeleton so hideous that even your closest friends have never been told what you did or what you said? Many of you are dealing with secrets that are so disturbing they taint your life like a cup of coffee filled with saccharin. There is a bitter aftertaste that all who involve themselves with you experience. It is not intentional. It is the sad consequences of too many secrets buried too deeply and never resolved. Have you ever had a guilty stain that time will not erase? Things in your past that seem to bleed through every success and accomplishment you have ever had? Could it be possible that in spite of your debauchery God could still love you? Perhaps I am being a bit too personal. Maybe it would be wiser to continue with Hosea's story. I just hope that somewhere, interwoven in the lines, you might extract a morsel of wisdom. Listen carefully.

Had this story occurred today, it would have been in every tabloid in the nation. It would be the butt of jokes for every comedian who needed material for stand-up comedy. How utterly ridiculous that this nobleman, this up-and-coming preacher, this world-renowned evangelist, would find himself enamored of a tramp. No matter how ridiculous it may seem, it was nonetheless true. He had fallen in love with a lady of the night. Can you imagine the jeering of the other prophets when he approached them? How could this great preacher walk with dignity holding this woman on his arm? Can you imagine the elderly ladies drinking tea and discussing how disappointing it was for this young man marked for greatness to ruin his career? Though he heard their remarks and felt the hot glare of their penetrating sneer, he was helpless to stop it. He was in love with her. Love numbs the senses to reason and intoxicates the consciousness of public opinion.

As ridiculous as it may seem to you, Hosea married Gomer. Holy matrimony indeed. What was holy about this matrimony? How can he hope to have a holy matrimony with an unholy thing? Yet he made her his wife. He gave her his name. He betrothed her his worldly goods. He gave her the benefit of his legacy. He wrapped around her bruised, battered shoulders the cloak of integrity. He washed the musky scent of other men's lust off her sensitive skin. He made her somebody. What can erase abuse? you ask. What will enable the besmirched to be washed clean? His love did it. He took her off the streets and into his home. He completely relocated her. He brought her into the neighborhoods that she had never been allowed into. He wanted to make her a lady. It was his desire to warm her heart and insulate her from the cold. He kissed away the pain of the shameful things she had done and never told anyone. He wrapped his arms around her and held her in the night until the trembling stopped, and she snuggled up against him as if she would be there forever—but she was not.

You see, when we have come from sordid pasts and damaged backgrounds, we tend to recoil when we are offered the unfamiliar kindness of love and tranquillity. It is amazing that when we have perceived our lives to be bad we have a tendency to feel uncomfortable with the adoration of that which seems good. I believe it is because we innately disagree with those who admire us. This is the sad consequence of low self-esteem. We have the tendency to cleave to the negative and oppose those who see us positively.

Gomer began to pull away from Hosea. Oh, you could not tell it initially, but little by little she drifted away. She stayed out too long. She didn't come back from the market for hours. He noticed that faraway look returning in her eyes. He knew that the last time he held her she seemed strangely distant. She was saying the same words, but the intensity had lessened and the passion had dissipated. He thought to himself that he caught the faint aroma of other men on her, but he dared not allow himself to believe that he could invest so much and still be so disrespected. No man wants to think that his love has failed to be enough to hold her tightly. What a blow to his self-confidence and a mar on his self-esteem. Yet it could not be denied. Little by little she seemed distracted and uncomfortable in a comfortable place. As is often the case with people who have come from dysfunctional backgrounds, if they're not careful, they have a tendency to find the great blessing of life to be a bit too unfamiliar for their taste.

Hosea and Gomer had several children, but it was said that none of them resembled him. Seldom will men feel comfortable taking care of children they did not father, especially if they were conceived while the woman was supposed to be committed to them. Gomer nurtured the children in Hosea's house. She slept them in his bed. He fed them and clothed them. But they did not resemble him. Instead they resembled others in the neighborhood, and yet he was still so good to them. What is God trying to tell us about Himself? Is he not saying that many of the things we conceived were not born of Him, and yet He protects and provides for the things that were not born of His will and divine purpose? It is amazing that God is so good He even takes care of those offspring we bring home who were not fathered by Him. You know, the offspring that result from our infidelity and lack of focus. Think of

280

the many pursuits that we venture into without prayer. They are the children we had who were born of our flesh. It could be the jobs we took without seeking His counsel. The places we moved because someone else led us to do it. These could even include the decisions we made that were not born out of His purpose. God is so in love with us that He even takes care of our mistakes. It was in that same kindness that Hosea raised Gomer's illegitimate children.

Finally, Hosea comes home one day expecting to find Gomer there but she is nowhere to be found. Her clothes are still in the closet, and her belongings are on the dresser. Everything is in place, but she is gone. She has aborted herself from the comfortable womb of love to which she had been called and plummeted back to the abyss from which she arose. She is a victim of her past. She is snared like a caged animal. She lies trapped like a creature who could not resist the bait. She is chained to her yesterday like an abused animal chained to the back of a porch. Though she tries to go forward, she inevitably snaps back into the original crisis again.

Hosea rushes out to find Gomer and bring her home. How ridiculous that this prophet, who has already run the risk of the complete annihilation of his reputation, will sink to an even deeper level and take a lantern and run out into the night to search the streets looking for his wife. How can he explain to his friends that his love was not enough to keep her at home? A man shouldn't have to ask other men for the whereabouts of his wife. He should have known where she was, but he could not find her. She was not at home. She was out of her place. She was lost. "Have you seen her?" he cries. You can imagine someone saying to him, "Forget her. You're better off anyway." But there's something about love that will not forget. And so he runs from street to street with the cold feel of cobblestone beneath his feet and the brisk wind of eastern air blowing through his clothes. His voice cries through the night. It is the sound of desperation. It is the call of God to a lost and dying world. "Gomer, Gomer, I'm looking for you and I will not rest until I find you!" "What kind of love is this?" you ask. This is the love of God, a God that would break his rest, walk out of eternity, come in the person of Jesus Christ, and walk the streets of time crying out for us, the children who were lost, we who walked away. It is for us that He died. Not that He needs us—He is God without us—but He is in love with us in spite of our past.

The search was on. It is the search of a loving God who will go to all lengths to reach us. There is no measuring the length of His love. It reaches to the highest mountain, and it sinks to the lowest valley. When Hosea finally found Gomer she was in the lowest valley. She was in a deplorable state. She was a mere fragment of what she could have been. When he saw her, he almost fainted. His head began to spin. The bitter taste of bile rose up in his mouth. The ground seemed to slip beneath his feet. "Gomer?" he asked in amazement. She dropped her head in shame. Sometimes the destitute are too ashamed to be found.

Shameless Love

When Hosea found Gomer, she was not dressed in the fine clothing that he had given her. Her hair was in total disarray. Her nails were not manicured. She stood on the slave table in the marketplace. Her dress was torn. Her hair was tattered. Her skin was smudged. Her naked knees were trembling. Her dirty face was wet with tears. They had put his wife on the slave table, and they were auctioning her off as though she were worth nothing at all. The men were jeering and talking about her obscenely. But not Hosea; he was feeling around in his purse. He was willing to spend all that he had to buy her. Most men would have turned their head in disgust, but not Hosea; he was shamelessly in love with her.

> Then the LORD said to me, "Go again, love a woman [who] is loved by [her] husband, yet an adulteress, even as the LORD loves the sons of Israel, though they turn to other gods and love raisin cakes." So I bought her for myself for fifteen [shekels] of silver and a homer and a half of barley. Then I said to her, "You shall stay with me for many days. You shall not play the harlot, nor shall you have a man; so I will also be toward you." Hos. 3:1–3 (NAS)

The men laughed at Hosea. He must be a fool, they said. Who would pay so much for so little? He loved her, and before he would let her go back to what she was, before he would let her be chained to her past, before he would let her be sold back to slavery to obey the whims of every passing stranger in her city, he would redeem her.

That's what God does for us. We are the ones who have betrayed His confidence and abused His mercy and found ourselves traveling back down the same treacherous streets from which He had called us. That's what He does when we have created our own hell and burned in the flames from our own foolish mistakes. He does what others would not do. He still cares for us. When we have walked away from the right and fallen headfirst into the wrong, He still searches for us, and, in spite of the embarrassment, the shame, and the trauma, He loves us. He can hear the rattling of our skeletons hidden away in our closets. He has seen the foolish mistakes of our past. Anyone else would have said we were not worth it. But He emptied his pockets and said, "I'll go bankrupt before I let you go back." How could He do it? you ask. I cannot explain it. I only know His Word describes it as "passion." He is the ultimate lover. He loved us so much that He gave the ultimate gift to the ultimate sinners. He figuratively emptied his pockets. He is in love with you even in spite of your past.

One thing I want to emphasize is that it is not Gomer's past that is the star in the story. We have given too much attention to negatives in our lives and not enough to the positive influences that sustained us through the negative issues we have faced. The real award must go to Hosea, whose love has stolen the show. He loved her out of her past. That is the kind of love that only God can give. If it were left to man alone, he would forsake us. That is too much weight and responsibility for you to ask of anyone but God. Only He has the kind of passion to love you out of your past and present you to others whole. Only He can redeem you out of your past and recapture your future.

Many of you are tormented by issues that haunt you. These scars cause your heart to wrench in pain. Yet you must understand through this illustrated sermon what God used Hosea to declare. He loves beyond the mistakes of our past. He is not like men who categorize us and have evaluated our future based on our past. He is a God who believes in the least likely and invests in the faltering. See His confidence in you, and let it give you the strength to believe in yourself.

Caution, God Is at Work

Oh, I must tell you, Hosea got his wife. He brought her off the table, but he got her back home again. He paid enough for her that he could have made her his slave, but he said, "Not my slave, you are my wife and I am your husband." And, little by little with the careful stitching of a shrewd tailor, he sewed her broken heart back together and rebuilt her self-esteem. He healed her thoughts. He touched her past. He reestablished what life had demolished. You see, He is the Lord of our past.

If you ever need Him to stitch you back, mend you, or restore you from the trauma of abuse, divorce, or some other esteem-demolishing issue, allow time for reconstruction. It might be best to hang out a sign that warns suitors, CAUTION, GOD IS AT WORK. Too many times, I have seen ladies who rushed through the healing and reopened the old wounds. You are literally a construction site until He refurbishes you. There will be debris and clutter that He will be clearing away for some time. But when all is said and done, you will be, as Gomer's name suggests, "complete."

And ye are complete in him, which is the head of all principality and power . . .   Col. 2:10

You might wonder why I've taken the time to laboriously depict the old and ancient love that is hidden within the chronicles of this Old Testament saga. There is a reason that I share this with you. This is a rare opportunity for God to teach us something that we can never fully understand. He wants you to know how much He is available to love you out of your past. This is a job for the Lord. You will find no human husband who has the ability to fix the broken areas of your past. Many men faint when they recognize that they are saddled down with unresolved issues. When they have to prove themselves because of what other men did, they become bitter and sullen, but not God. He will empty out His pockets so that He can heal you before He presents you to anyone else to love. He has declared that we will never know the height and depth and breadth and the length of His love. But it is awesome to catch a small glimpse of its splendor in this love story.

Now, I do not know what happened to you. I don't know where you were or whom you were with. I cannot see the many incidents and accidents and traumas you have survived. But I wonder, does the fragrance of your cologne mask the odor of your past? I can almost hear the muffled cry of abused children whose childhood issues are now buried beneath silk dresses and designer bags. If I listen carefully, I can hear the cry of women who have been raped in the night and sworn to secrecy in the light. If I look closely, I can almost detect the falling tears that leak from pain-filled eyes in the middle of the night. I can see the trail they leave as they cross the bridge of your nose and plummet quietly to your pillow. None of us can change what we were, where we were, or whose we were before. But it is important to understand that the God who knows our deepest secret has already searched the skeleton in our closets and still loves us. He loves us so perfectly that when others smirked and laughed and jeered and saw us on the slave table, He decided, "I still want you." Though many men have touched you, life has abused you, women have mishandled you, circumstances betrayed you, He still wants you. As horrendous as your past may seem to you and to those around you, He needs you to know that He is the Lord of your past.

My recommendation to you is to forget those things that are behind and reach to those things that are before you. I recommend that you run as fast as you can into your future and away from your adversity. I challenge you to take the wings of the morning and sail toward your destiny. I challenge you to embark upon new horizons. Settle down into this season in your life. No more running back into your past. You are free. This time you are to stand firm and unmoved. There will be no turning back.

> Awake, awake, O Zion, clothe yourself with strength. Put on your garments of splendor, O Jerusalem, the holy city. The uncircumcised and defiled will not enter you again. Shake off your dust; rise up, sit enthroned, O Jerusalem. Free yourself from the chains on your neck, O captive Daughter of Zion. For this is what the LORD says: "You were sold for nothing, and without money you will be redeemed." Isa. 52:1–3 (NIV)

Awake, O captive daughter of Zion, break the bands off of your necks, for whom the Son sets free is free indeed! In the same way that God delivers Israel, He will deliver you. You are free from your past, released from your failures, and challenged by your future. There is a better day waiting on you. If you can forgive yourself and accept His forgiveness, there is nothing about your yesterday that can circumvent your tomorrow. Reach out! God has a blessing for you. Reach beyond the memories, the pain, and the past. The future is before you. The best of life awaits you. You can have it. Take life to your bosom and hold it in your arms. Reach out and take a second chance. It is yours today because of His shameless love.

Chapter Fourteen

Serving the Lord and Making the Money

N o one can serve two masters. Either
he will hate the one and love the other,
or he will be devoted to the one and
despise the other. You cannot serve both
God and Money.

Matt. 6:24 (NIV)

God doesn't mind you making the
money. He minds you serving it. That is to
say, you are not to yield your praise and
presence toward it as if you think that having wealth is the answer to the questions of
life. It certainly is not. It does not replace

love, family, or spirituality. It is the foolish idea of the acquisition of things bringing fulfillment that God hates. It is a lie. It does not bring fulfillment.

However, we must admit that having financial strength does enhance us if we are well rounded in other areas. Money is like makeup. It doesn't make the woman, but she sure looks better when she has it well applied and amply bestowed. For all of our modern coyness about Christians and finance, the Bible is filled with text that teaches the balanced acquisition of economy. But we must always be careful that we acquire it without worshiping it. God is jealous. He will smite your career if it starts to take His place in your life. Woe to the woman who is too busy making money to worship God. God needs to be foremost in her mind, the priority in her life. Once that is established, He has promised to the one who sacrifices and gives to the kingdom many, many blessings. These are not just the blessings of heaven; He has promised to bless her now. You need to make sure that you include God in your financial planning, estate planning, and all other areas of business. He is the source; your job is just the means from which your blessing is derived. He will bless you a hundredfold if He knows you will not worship what He gives you.

> And Jesus answered and said, Verily I say unto you, There is no man that hath left house, or brethren, or sisters, or father, or mother, or wife, or children, or lands, for my sake, and the gospel's, But he shall receive an hundredfold now in this time, houses, and brethren, and sisters, and mothers, and children, and lands, with persecutions; and in the world to come eternal life.
>
> Mark 10:29–30

But I must warn you that blessings can bring persecution. Do not fail to understand that. People never attack mediocrity; it is greatness that they envy. No one attacks a bag lady. She can walk the most dangerous streets and not be robbed. It is the successful who are the most vulnerable to public venom and animosity. Yet do not shy away from money just because God says do not worship it and people do not want you to have it. If God chooses to bless you, take the persecution, my sister, and get the cash. It will enhance your life. It will give you options that poverty cannot afford. It will enable you to do things for the kingdom that the poor can only pray for.

> A feast is made for laughter, and wine makes life merry, but money is the answer for everything.
> Eccles. 10:19 (NIV)

It has been said that money is the answer to everything. It will assist you and enhance you with many things. Money can be a blessing, but it will not satisfy all areas. Temper your drive for money with your passion for God's presence, and you will ultimately be a woman who gets it all. The woman of excellence discussed in Proverbs 31 is a woman who manages to get it all. She maximizes her potentials, but she doesn't worship her ambitions. It is hard to strike that balance, but if you do, you can be a lady who wins the admiration of her spouse, the favor of her Lord, and the confidence in herself.

> She considereth a field, and buyeth it: with the fruit of her hands she planteth a vineyard. She girdeth her loins with strength, and strengtheneth her arms. She perceiveth that her merchandise

is good: her candle goeth not out by night. She layeth her hands to the spindle, and her hands hold the distaff. She stretcheth out her hand to the poor; yea, she reacheth forth her hands to the needy. She is not afraid of the snow for her household: for all her household are clothed with scarlet. She maketh herself coverings of tapestry; her clothing is silk and purple. Her husband is known in the gates, when he sitteth among the elders of the land. She maketh fine linen, and selleth it; and delivereth girdles unto the merchant. Strength and honour are her clothing; and she shall rejoice in time to come. She openeth her mouth with wisdom; and in her tongue is the law of kindness. She looketh well to the ways of her household, and eateth not the bread of idleness.

Prov. 31:16–27

This woman who is listed in the Scriptures as a virtuous woman is a woman of capabilities and resources. Some people say that Christianity is repressive of women. I do not believe this is true. I believe that some of the men who preach it may be repressive of women, but this is not the way of the Bible. In the Bible, a good woman is a strong character of great significance. When the Bible does defer position to the man, it is for the benefit of the woman that she might be spared the blistering plight of struggle and inclement conditions from which he is there to shield her. No, in the Bible, a virtuous woman is not weak. She is a creative, resourceful woman who is aggressive while still being feminine. She is relational with a man, but she is not with him because she lacks the skill to survive on her own. What a blessing it is for her to choose her companion based on his character and not his economy. When a woman chooses a husband based on his ability to provide alone, she may choose someone who is endowed financially but impoverished spiritually. A virtuous woman does choose someone who is successful, but also someone who is not intimidated by her success.

The virtuous woman of the Proverbs teaches two things. Number one, she encourages her sisters to maximize their opportunities, so they do not marry out of financial need. This lesson is significant because a successful man is attracted to women of worth and not women of weight. Women of weight are those who add little and require much. They are women who are hoping God will send someone to relieve them of their indebtedness and assume the weight of their oppression. Most men do not want to be viewed as a financial statement. They don't want a woman who needs to be saved from economic ruin and sees him as a lifeline. They go out of their way to avoid a woman who comes with financial baggage and brings nothing to add to the pot. If you do not add to his portfolio, that is fine, but please do not plan on being a burden and swapping sex for debt. Emulate the virtuous woman, and take care of yourself financially. Manage your bills so you are not a liability. A good woman doesn't want to be a liability. Even if circumstances have handed her a bad deal, she isn't looking to enter into a marital welfare arrangement. Follow her example and take care of your own.

The second thing a virtuous woman teaches is that a woman who has established herself economically would be wise to choose a mate who is just as successful in some area. It doesn't have to be the same area, but he needs a claim to fame. Then there is no jealousy or competition between them. She has her accomplishments, and he has his as well.

Of course, there are some men who, no matter how successful they are, do not have the self-esteem to support a successful lady. A man needs to be sure of himself. If he is great but doesn't acknowledge his own greatness, soon he will not acknowledge yours. He has to be a man who is assured without being arrogant. Many women are suffering today because they are stifled by relationships with men who do not enjoy women's ability to achieve. A man is often intimidated, either because she insists on flaunting her success before him or, more often than not, he is insecure. Choose your mate carefully, so you know he will celebrate your success and not hold you down.

> Her husband is known in the gates, when he sitteth among the elders of the land.   Prov. 31:23

If you are not yet married, take a long, intense look at the one whom you are planning to marry, especially if you see yourself as a woman who will inevitably rise into a position of success and accomplishments. Make sure you're with a man who not only understands your desire to achieve but who is proud of it as well. If you are already the queen of the corporation you run, you would do well to leave your job and your superior demeanor at work. Few men will feel comfortable if you dominate in the home. Yet it is difficult for the woman who is used to being in charge to know where the boundaries end. Pay careful attention and take heed not to step on any toes. Make your home a haven where your accomplishments will be publicly praised, respected, and appreciated.

A virtuous woman can manage to have it all. She is a force in her own right. She is strong enough to survive on her own, but she chooses not to do so. This woman will not manipulate a relationship because she is so endowed through her walk with God that she may want to have a man in her life, but she does not need to have him. God has shown her how to manage her life. He has shown her how to choose a man who is not intimidated and who can enter into her life feeling wanted rather than just needed. Do you want to be a woman of virtue? It's hard work, but believe me, it is worth it.

There seems to be a myth of poverty attached to Christianity. Many people, Christians and non-Christians alike, view accumulating wealth as un-Christian behavior. There's a tendency to think that the Christian must dress like a monk and live in a monastery, or he or she is not sincere. Well, I bring a message of liberation. The Lord does not mean for you to forsake all ambitions in order to serve Him. He just wants to be your priority.

> This Book of the Law shall not depart from your mouth, but you shall meditate in it day and night, that you may observe to do according to all that is written in it. For then you will make your way prosperous, and then you will have good success.
>
> Josh. 1:8 (NKJ)

The virtuous woman was a very wealthy, progressive woman. The Bible applauds her, but not for her wealth alone; her extreme balance is her greatest achievement. Her balance makes her the ideal role model for the modern woman. She was spiritual, and still she was successful. She was maternal, and yet she was career oriented. She was independent, but she was relational. This is the success that comes from having a Christ-centered life. When you seek Him first and make Him the top priority in your life, success in all things will follow. He must be

302

the goal that you strive for. If He is, He will accessorize your life with fullness and completeness that is totally different from that which we can do apart from Him. You do not want the kind of success that wrecks your home, gives you ulcers, and drives you into mad obsessions. You want your blessings to come from your relationship with the Lord. This is the kind of wealth that does not leave you addicted to a career and denied someone with whom to share it. True success, the kind that enhances your life and makes you a better person in every way, can come only from God.

> The blessing of the LORD, it maketh
> rich, and he addeth no sorrow with it.
> Prov. 10:22

Please know that this is more than a statement suggesting you are to be prosperous. It is a message suggesting that true prosperity is the balanced blessing of God in every area of your life. You can have it all, if you seek Him first. It is His pleasure to give you everything that you need. He does not mind you having things. He just doesn't want material things to have you. The Christian woman has for years had to fight through false messages that suggested her place was in the home. But that is not Biblical. You are welcome to stay at home, if you feel that you are called to be a domestic goddess. But if you are so inclined to impact your community and your society by working, God is with you in your ambition. The fine print stipulated only that He is first place in your life. He wants to be first above your business, your companion, and all else that you aspire to attain. A person can be financially successful and still be a good Christian, as long as the Lord is first in her life. In fact, the principle of tithing is merely a person refusing to exclude her success from her worship. When someone recognizes the Lord as the source, she brings the tithe to Him as a means of honoring Him above the tangibles that she has received. It is her way of saying, "Lord, you are first place in my life!"

> Therefore take no thought, saying, What shall we eat? or, What shall we drink? or, Wherewithal shall we be clothed? (For after all these things do the Gentiles seek:) for your heavenly Father knoweth that ye have need of all these things. But seek ye first the kingdom of God, and his righteous-

ness; and all these things shall be added unto you. Take therefore no thought for the morrow: for the morrow shall take thought for the things itself. Sufficient unto the day is the evil thereof. Matt. 6:31–34

The lady who wants balance is too wise to seek riches. She knows that the pursuit of tangibles does not bring fulfillment. But just because she doesn't make material things the goal of her life does not mean that she doesn't know how to maximize the blessings that are fringe benefits of her making God first. That's right, "these things" that Matthew 6:33 refers to are fringe benefits. When a woman makes the Lord her pursuit, she then is eligible for all of the benefits that are derived from seeking Him first. This truth is illustrated in the story of Solomon in I Kings. Solomon proved that his motives were pure when he asked God for wisdom, and God said He would throw in wealth just because Solomon's priorities were aligned with His purpose.

And the speech pleased the Lord, that Solomon had asked this thing. And God said unto him, Because thou hast asked this thing, and hast not asked for thyself long life; neither hast asked riches for thyself, nor hast asked the life of thine enemies; but hast asked for thyself understanding to discern judgment; Behold, I have done according to thy words: lo, I have given thee a wise and an understanding heart; so that there was none like thee before thee, neither after thee shall any arise like unto thee. And I have also given thee that which thou hast not asked, both riches, and honour: so that there shall not be any among the kings like unto thee all thy days.

I Kings 3:10–13

A wise woman does not seek advancement from men or from God. She knows that her economic strength is not dependent on marrying the right man. Nor does she have to spend her entire life chasing riches. She seeks only the presence of God, and He then gives her the things she desires. When the wise woman seeks a husband, she chooses on the basis of his character and not his financial portfolio. She wants a man who is secure enough to feel comfortable with her success. But by no means does she need him to fulfill her financial dreams. She has her future wrapped up in her relationship with God.

Eve, the Mother of Creation

The woman was called to assist the Master in the creative process of childbirth. What a calling! By her very nature, woman is creative. She carries dreams in the womb of her mind and gives birth to ideas that will bring life to her family and her finances. Creativity is yet another gift God has given his daughters. You must use it to its full potential. The virtuous woman knows that through the grace of the Lord she was granted the ability to create, to be the force that brings forth great children and great ideas, a happy home and a life of riches. She knows she must make use of that special gift as God intended. She doesn't sit around waiting for things to happen; she makes them happen. No, she doesn't go chasing riches; she knows that by seeking God, He will take care of her. But she also knows that He is taking care of her by giving her the gifts of thought and creativity. What she does with those gifts is up to her.

The virtuous woman is an asset to whoever knows her. She is a pillar of strength. She has vision, and she is endowed with the ability to bring that vision to life. She is not some ditzy airhead who walks around with her face looking up to heaven and her feet tripping over the earth. She is a woman who makes the most of her life. That is what the Lord wants for His daughters. He wants you to maximize your life. He does not want you to spend your life waiting for anyone or anything to come along. If you are still sitting in the tower waiting for Prince Charming to come riding in on a white horse and pick up your hanky, I strongly suggest that you climb down those steps, pick up your own hanky, and enjoy your life. I am not saying he isn't coming. I am just saying that in the meantime you are wasting precious time. When he does come, he is far more apt to be attracted to a woman whose life and finances are not stuck up a tree!

Yes, I will admit that many men enjoy a woman who acts a little helpless. It makes us feel needed. But there is a difference between a woman who acts helpless and one who really is helpless. We all want to associate with people who are an asset and not a liability. So before you demand a prince, be sure that you are at least a princess. Cinderella stories do not happen often. That's why they're fairy tales and read to people who want to dream. But if you want to live your dream instead of sleep through it, you might do better to get busy and turn your little mop into a cleaning service. Then you can buy your own glass slipper!

Creativity begins with a healthy respect for your own opinions and thoughts. I want you to rise every morning and thank God for your creativity. Thank Him for the thoughts you need to solve the problems you have. I know you might not feel like you have the solutions, but have faith in God and in yourself and the answers will come. You and God are the tag team that wins the fights and takes home the trophy. Many people have self-confidence and no faith in God. Others have faith in God but none in themselves. But a balanced person knows that both are necessary, and through Him you will find your way.

I can do all things through Christ which strengtheneth me.   Phil. 4:13

When Paul says, "I can do all things," that's self-confidence. Then he says, "Through

Christ which strengtheneth me," and that is faith in God. He acknowledges his relationship with the Lord as his secret edge. It strengthens him. Allow the Lord to strengthen you as you enjoy your life and the many challenges that it brings.

Since self-confidence and God-confidence are so vital, let's take a deeper look into these two areas. Self-confidence is all about self-perception. How do you view yourself? Now, self-perception is not always based in reality. Some of the smartest people in the world might think they're dumb, and the guy who is as ignorant as a tree stump can convince himself, and everyone else, that he really knows what he is talking about. The funny thing is, you actually become what you think you are. If you see yourself as incompetent, you will never really succeed.

You see, it doesn't matter whether you're really incompetent or not. If you think that you are a failure, you will be one. So how do these self-perceptions come about? They are usually taught to us. Our parents, our teachers, people we look up to are our mirrors reflecting an image of ourselves back at us. Compliments, praise, and encouragement help us develop a positive self-image. But criticism, hurtful words, and cruel lies damage us beyond repair. Abuse and trauma cripple us in ways that leave no outward scars. It is less debilitating to be physically crippled than to be crippled in your self-perception. I have known many women who are physically challenged and are productive individuals who enjoy their lives. Though they are incapacitated physically, they refuse to allow negativity to creep into their self-esteem. By the same token, we have all known women who had everything going for them but did not know it. They are emotional invalids, dysfunctional and miserable. These women were cursed into living in the shadows. They are haunted by ghosts and imaginary restrictions. They are tied to the dungeons of invisible obstacles. They are always needy and desperate, often promiscuous and seldom committed. They are so thirsty for help because they have not discovered their own resources. Anytime you do not see yourself as a resource, you constantly search for someone to draw from. That drawing becomes a drain, and like an automobile whose lights have been left on, you eventually dry out all those who are close to you, until finally the relationships stall.

> Now unto him that is able to do exceeding abundantly above all that we ask or think, according to the power that worketh in us . . .   Eph. 3:20

The Bible says that God uses the "power that worketh within us." He doesn't just use what is within us. He uses the "power that worketh" within us. Suppose that power within you is lying dormant and untapped because you don't recognize your own resources? What if your self-esteem is so low that you don't see any of the gifts within you, so you don't use them? What would God have to work with then? How can He help you if you don't help yourself? That is why we must take the time to be spiritually rejuvenated. It is essential that you are functioning at optimum capacity. You are going to need a full charge in your battery, so you can be productive and creative. Whatever you do, you must not allow anyone or anything to rob you of your faith in yourself.

Now, having said that, you must also have faith in God. Why is that important? Because only through God will you find greatness. Many secular women have strong wills and self-esteem; they believe in their own strength and inner ability. But they eventually run into a challenge for which they are poorly equipped. There are some things that are beyond the scope of human might or force. There are some obstacles that will confront you and require more than positive attitude. These challenges require a resolute, unshakable faith in God. When you face a challenge that you are not equipped to handle, you basically have two choices. First, you can shrink back into the safety of your self-controlled accomplishments. For the secular woman, this is the only option, for she has nowhere else to turn. She has only faith in herself, yet this challenge is beyond her abilities, so she must run away from it. However, if you are a Christian woman, you have a second option. You can turn to God, reach out to Him, and trust in Him for a miracle. He is the God who can do what you cannot. No wonder Paul said, "I can do all things through Christ which strengtheneth me." He knew that he and God together were a force too mighty to be defeated.

Now, I must say this to you: when God blesses you with creative thought, the thought is not for your enjoyment; it is for your edification. That means it comes to build you up. It will not build you up if you do not do what you are thinking. Creative thought without faith-filled action will leave you a dreamer. You will be a resource center for other people who take your ideas and move to the top. If you are woman enough to create the concept, then be woman enough to produce the product. If you do not act upon your ideas, you will always be a "Janey-come-lately," who becomes bitter because others acted on what you thought. God blesses what you think, but He praises what you do.

> And he shall be like a tree planted by the rivers of water, that bringeth forth his fruit in his season; his leaf also shall not wither; and whatsoever he doeth shall prosper. Ps. 1:3

Write this Scripture down, especially if you have been the kind of woman who tends to lapse into "dream state" faith and fails to act on what you have been given. Just personalize it and say it this way:

AND (PLACE YOUR NAME) SHALL BE LIKE A TREE PLANTED BY THE RIVERS OF WATERS; HER LEAF ALSO SHALL NOT WITHER AND WHATSO EVER (PLACE YOUR NAME HERE) DOETH SHALL PROSPER!

Write it, read it, believe it, and do it!

So, as a Christian woman, how can you

activate the power of God to assist you in accomplishing the things you cannot do for yourself?

STEP ONE: Realize that financial strength is not the first pursuit.

STEP TWO: Realize that God will not move where there is no faith in Him.

STEP THREE: Realize that God will use something that you already have within.

STEP FOUR: Look within yourself and acknowledge the gifts with which God has graced you.

STEP FIVE: Use the gifts He has given you, but remember that God is the giver of ideas. He doesn't hand out checks, nor does He let dollars rain down from heaven. He gives thoughts and the gift of creativity; what you do with them is your gift to Him.

STEP SIX: Act upon those gifts, or those gifts will not act for you. It is not enough to acknowledge your gifts; you must act on them to achieve your dreams and goals. Do it, do it, and do it!

STEP SEVEN: Give God the glory when you achieve your accomplishments. Remember that God will give you all that you need. But when you achieve, take no credit for yourself. Always acknowledge Him.

Now a certain woman of the wives of the sons of the prophets cried out to Elisha, "Your servant my husband is dead, and you know that your servant feared the LORD; and the creditor has come to take my two children to be his slaves." And Elisha said to her, "What shall I do for you? Tell me, what do you have in the house?" And she said, "Your maidservant has nothing in the house except a jar of oil." Then he said, "Go, borrow vessels at large for yourself from all your neighbors, [even] empty vessels; do not get a few. And you shall go in and shut the door behind you and your sons, and pour out into all these vessels; and you shall set aside what is full." So she went from him and shut the door behind her and her sons; they were bringing [the vessels] to her and she poured. And it came about when the vessels were full, that she said to her son, "Bring me another vessel." And he said to her, "There is not one vessel more." And the oil stopped. Then she came and told the man of God. And he said, "Go, sell the oil, and pay your debt, and you [and] your sons can live on the rest."

II Kings 4:1–7 (NAS)

Every point that I have discussed in this chapter is somewhere in this woman's story. She was so poor that she was about to lose her sons to enslavement. She was overwhelmed and distraught by her bills. She blames her dilemma on the absence of a man. However, she is about to discover the power of God. She acknowledges first of all that she is the wife of a prophet, and thereby we realize that she is a woman who has pursued God and God alone. Yet, having pursued Him, she is still unsure of how to take the faith that she has and use it to change her economy. When the prophet commands her to go borrow vessels, she proves that she has faith; she acts on what he has commanded her to do. Can you imagine it? She is already in debt up to her ears, and Elisha tells her to go borrow. Part of her faith has come from the fact that at this point she has nothing to lose. Her strength alone has already proven to be not enough to accomplish financial well-being. She needs divine help. Now, notice that the man of God shows her how to use what she already has. That is the value of good ministry. Good ministry shows you how to activate what you already have within. He asks her, "What do you have in your house?" That is a significant question. It is a question we should all ask ourselves. You must always know what you have. It is not enough to know what others have; you will not be freed by what someone else has. You will be empowered only by what you have. Like this woman of the Bible, you have resources that God can use to bless you economically. He will empower those that He can trust. No matter what you have received, always remember Him. He will continue to direct you and empower you with more and more creativity. I hope you are motivated to start to exercise your God-given resources and become a woman of action. As He begins to release creativity in you and you see Him open door after door in your behalf, always remember to honor Him. How can you acknowledge him? Simply tell anyone who asks you that your secret weapon is your relationship with your Lord. That is all He wants from you. It is that simple and yet many fail to remember. Please do not forget it. Your next financial decision is predicated on your ability to honor Him for your last one. Do not fear the future. The future cannot harm you. Are you ready for your next thought, gift, or instruction? This is how you receive it.

> In all your ways acknowledge him,
>   and he will make your paths
>   straight.
> Do not be wise in your own eyes;
>   fear the LORD and shun evil.
> This will bring health to your body
>   and nourishment to your bones.
> Honor the LORD with your wealth,
>   with the first fruits of all your
>   crops; then your barns will be filled
>   to overflowing, and your vats will
>   brim over with new wine.
>   Prov. 3:6–10 (NIV)

Chapter Fifteen

Now I Lay Me Down
to Sleep

Every woman who walks with God walks
through storms, winds, and rain. Her life is
filled with challenges and victories. She is
like the anointing oil that was mixed by the
apothecary. She is a careful blend of life's
many spices. Her personality is a potpourri
of so many different things that years of
knowing her will not disclose all that makes
her who she is. She is carefully concocted
and slowly simmered, stirred patiently by her
Lord. It is amazing how patient God is in
preparing her for her destiny. He knows how
long it takes. He knows whom to send into

her life. He knows what events it will take to bring her to a place of maturity in Him. He is emphatically her Lord.

It will not take her long to realize that though she may have many admirers, friends, and family, none will ever take the place of her Lord. His place in her life is the foundation of every success she will ever have. He will be there in every moment of pain and glory. He is the thing that brings her life together. It is His love for her that kept her mind from breaking under the stress of life, and when all is said and done, no one could hold her like He can. She will be prosperous in her business, successful in her relationships, contented in her personhood, but it is all because of Him. It is knowing Him that gives her the grace to endure transitions, to withstand opposition, and to know that when the day ends, it is He who watches her through the night and His kiss that takes her out of her sleep come dawn. He is her Lord.

Oh, yes, it is a privilege to know and love, hold and touch a lady of excellence. It is an honor to be born out of her womb. It is a distinct privilege to hold her hand in marriage, feel her warm body wrapped in warm blankets in the middle of the night. It is delightful to hear the tinkling sound of the laughter that comes from the mouth of a woman whose heart is filled with love and peace. We watch her like admirers in a museum. We appreciate her like connoisseurs of fine cuisine. But, when all is said and done, there is a part of her life that none can touch but her Lord.

We Are No Competition, for He Is the Man

For thy Maker is thine husband; the LORD of hosts is his name; and thy Redeemer the Holy One of Israel; The God of the whole earth shall he be called.   Isa. 54:5

No one can compare to Him. He knows how to be with you and comfort you like no human ever can. That is not to say that there is no place for us men in your life, but it is to admit that His place can never be ours. If I have learned anything at all, it is the importance of knowing one's limitations. For no one can determine their areas of strength without knowing their areas of weakness. It is the realization that all flesh will fail and all humans will disappoint that makes us all need God. We will have passion. We will have pain. We will have sunshine and moments of rain. It is understanding this that gives us the flexibility to accept the many seasons that come to all of our lives. I have learned to know my place.

The man's place in the life of his wife is to walk beside her and to be her friend. To listen and to laugh and to enjoy the many stages and ages that we walk through together. It is realizing that we walk a winding road through rugged terrain, struggling and stumbling but pressing forward, that makes us understand the only real compass we have is the Lord. If a man could understand his limitations in her life, he will love his lady and then release her to find the ultimate fulfillment in the arms of the Lord. A man cannot be jealous of God. There are simply some things that God can do that a man never can. If a man loves a woman, he will help her find Him. God is the source of ultimate fulfillment of which we are merely a shadow. He is the ultimate physician who heals the scars that life inflicts. It is His whispered words of wisdom that cause her finally to rest at night. It is the assurance of His presence that eases the many sorrows that life will bring before her. Never be jealous. Never compete. For her Lord is your Lord. And the closer she gets to Him, the more whole she is with you.

I have learned to lay me down to sleep. And I have learned to pray for the Lord to keep the many things that are beyond me. I need only look up to Him and His smile to know that no matter what challenges I face, He alone is the one who gives the grace I need to persevere, to go on, and to succeed. The art of being a virtuous woman's lover is to understand completely that you cannot be her Lord.

If I Should Die Before I Wake

We never know what the next second will bring to us. Every time we hear a knock at the door, we run to answer it with uncertainty. We do not know who is on the other side. When we sit calmly in our homes and have that calmness disrupted by the shrill sound of a ringing telephone, we answer it never knowing how the call may change our lives. We meet strangers without the benefit of seeing how each meeting will affect our destiny. Life is just so uncertain.

It was one of those uncertainties that swept me and my wife into a new experience. It was not an experience that we enjoyed, but it was one that we have endured. We both staggered beneath the weight of it and wrestled to make sense of it. But we were thankful that we knew the Lord through it all. I would like to elaborate on this challenge. I do it with the intent that you might better realize how significant it is to have a stabilizing force in the midst of the changing winds of life. I must tell you there have been many times through the years that we have survived painful moments because we have seen what others could not see. We are not perfect, nor are we martyrs for a cause, just weary people stumbling down a winding road, grasping onto promises, groping toward truth, but having received help from God, we continue on.

I mentioned earlier the passing of my wife's mother. It was to me one of the most tragic experiences of my adult life. It was a tragedy because I realized that a wonderful woman had slipped away from us. It was also a tragedy because in the passing of her mother, a piece of my wife had slipped away.

I saw it in her eyes. Her vibrant gaze was replaced by an empty stare. Who can describe the aching sting of death? Its venom had invaded our lives and altered our momentum, and we were left trying to regain the rhythm that had once seemed so easy to maintain.

I can still smell the strong odor of disinfectant that invaded our nostrils as we sat in the intensive care waiting room. It had become our hotel of agony as we waited for each new report, each new doctor's prognosis. The constant hum of the respirator accompanied us during the visiting hours. In the waiting room, the blaring television that no one seemed to be really watching kept us company. We sat numbly, looking into space, while endless talk-show hosts took deeper and deeper voyages into the abyss of human corruption and debauchery. It did not matter to us who cheated on her boyfriend with a best friend. We didn't need the shock-value trash that some people call entertainment. We were living in the middle of an overbudget, understaffed drama that seemed more like a horror story than anything else. So we sat waiting to see how the movie ended, fearing the worst but hoping for the best. We sat there trying to distract ourselves from the thick blanket of worry that wrapped itself around us. Yet in spite of our prayers and spiritual training, it seemed that each of us knew that this was a formidable foe. We tried not to think of what it would mean if the Lord decided to take away the life of someone we held precious.

I have always prided myself on being strong in a crisis. I always felt it was my job to make things as nice as possible and provide support for my wife and our family. After all, I was the man, the one who promised to be there through thick and thin. But what do you do when being there seems to make no difference? What can you say when words seem hollow and assurances sound ridiculous? I tell you what you do: you sit there and begin to realize the vast difference between the role you play as her lover and the limitations that are involved in real crises.

In the hospital bed, my mother-in-law seemed to stare at me with big questioning eyes. It was the look she always gave me when she was concerned and needed my advice. I served as her pastor as well as her son. She had always respected me. She thought I could do anything, but this was a bit too much for the ol' boy. I hated the helpless feeling that swirled around in the base of my stomach. Little did I know that my pain was for your gain, that through my crisis a ministry would be completed. I was in school, and I didn't even know it. You see, that is all life is. It is one big, endless school that withholds its diploma until the class is over.

Mother, as I had always called her—partially to distinguish her from my mom whom, though I am grown, I still call Momma—seemed stronger. She had a great day, and we were all served a large slice of optimism. She smiled that day and responded to jokes with smiles and silent laughs. Though she couldn't speak because of the hideous-looking tubes that were pumping her oxygen and assisting her lungs that were too weak to work, it was still apparent she was glad to be surrounded by her family. I left the hospital feeling hopeful.

But by the next day, Mother took a turn for the worse and, after a few hours, had lapsed into an unconscious state. My wife aged before me like a character in a movie who is made up for a role that she is too young to play. Later that day, I knew, as she turned the corner and entered the waiting room, that this was a dark moment in our lives. She told me to come and say good-bye, that her mother was slipping away. It wasn't long before my wife's mother had stared far beyond where my human eyes could see and went through a curtain to a place that I have often preached of but never have seen. She was gone, and we were left alone with her body in a room that suddenly seemed as quiet as a crypt. She was gone like vapors into air. She passed through the room like wind passes through the trees. She had vanished from everywhere but our minds. There was nothing left of her but fleeting memories and scant pictures of moments that had suddenly become more valuable because we all knew that they could never be repeated.

I had seen my wife sleep in waiting rooms, walk hospital floors, and try to meet every need that her mother had. I still remember when she laid her head on my chest and whispered, "My mother is gone." I can still hear her pain-filled cries. Her wailing voice will echo in my heart the rest of my life. I have never known the kind of helplessness that I felt that day. I have never felt more incompetent and incapable than I did in that one fleeting moment.

I searched frantically through my mind for something that I could do to ease her pain as I fought desperately to swallow my own. I thought that as a man I was expected to fix every problem that arises in the family, but I had never felt so limited and insufficient. I looked at the telephone, trying to think of someone who I could call, but there was no one who could fix this. No human contact could eradicate the trauma of this moment. It is at times like these that we realize neither friends, stock, nor capital gain can assist with real-life issues. No credit card could erase the debt and the deficit that was left in the room that suddenly became so silent. There were no great words of wisdom that erupted from my lips that day. No oratorical ability or skill would wipe away the pain that swept my wife's face, and suddenly I recognized how desperately each of us needed the Lord. You see, we will never discover God's greatness until we look our weakness straight in the face and conclude that there has to be someone bigger than you and I are.

I held my wife as if she were a child. I took care of all the funeral arrangements and answered all the polite condolences that flooded in from all over the country. I tried to assure my wife that I had everything in control. I threw all of my energy into preparing for the funeral, all the while wishing I could have done something to prevent it rather than prepare for it. My wife seemed as limp as a wet dishrag. Conversing with her became difficult. She really wasn't listening. She was in such pain that I hurt for her. I had seen her birth children, undergo surgery, endure emotional pain, survive financial plights, and overcome all other struggles, but I had never seen her as languid as she was in the weeks and months that followed.

In Need of the Lord

I must tell you how I fought through the coming weeks to distract her from her grief. I foolishly thought that if I was ardent and sensitive, compassionate and available, I could somehow distract her from the absence of her mother. I tried to cover every detail, so she would have everything she needed. I was determined to give her so much husband and so much love that she would not even realize that a major piece of her life had slipped away. I finally realized how foolish this was, but not before I had swept her across the country. I tried to swoon her on sandy beaches, singing songs, writing poetry, buying gifts, all in some mad need to fill an aching void that I could see behind her eyes. And though she smiled and tried to entertain me with polite conversation, I still noticed her frequent walks to the window in the middle of the night. I noticed how she stared out into the darkness. I knew she could see nothing through the window, and yet she was looking at something all the while. She was looking at something that I could not see. She remembered thoughts that I could not remember. She looked out of the window of our bedroom into her childhood and saw birthday cakes that I never ate. Tricycles that I never rode. And Easter bunnies that were not made for me. Her pain was too personal to be shared. And suddenly I recognized that although I love her deeply, I could only stand back and watch her. You see, there are some things that you will face alone. There are no spectators, and crowds are not allowed. Even husbands cannot help. It is at these times that you must have a relationship with the Lord.

I lay in the bed beside her, wrapped my strong arms around her, kissed her shoulder gently, and tried to make her secure, hoping that she would sleep. But I realized that my arms were not broad enough or strong enough to reach the part of her that needed to be held. I bought roses and played music for her. I took her out to dinner. I tried comedy and intimacy. I failed miserably. I realize now that there are some states of grief that she didn't want to be rescued from. She wanted to remember and laugh and cry. That was her memorial to her mother's legacy. It reaffirmed the absolute importance of her mother and it was her desperate attempt to hold on to her.

It took me weeks to realize that nothing I said, sang, wrote, or did would sufficiently numb the pain that she felt, that neither I nor the children nor all of our many friends could replace what she had lost. It was then that I learned the greatest respect for grief. It was then that I realized that grief is a process that cannot be aborted. In those weeks and months that followed, I began to understand why God created time. Time is a great healer. It is slow, but it is effective. And none of us can rush it. We must leave it to meander along at its own pace. And although we are all together on this planet, when it comes to real crisis, we are all somehow left tragically alone, with nothing but time and God to heal us.

He Woke Me Up This Morning

During that painful time, I found out the difference between the lover and the Lord. You see, it takes a real crisis for us to recognize that even the most agile of us will stumble and flounder through the changing tempos of life. Life does change tempos from time to time. We never know which rhythm it is going to take. I had always felt good about dancing with my partner, but now keeping up with the changes of life was another issue altogether. Now I found myself stumbling to regain some footing. The music was racing forward, and she was falling down in pain. I thought I could help her, but my feet were frozen to the floor. She needed me, so I tried to wave my hand magically, but there was no magic in my fingers—not for this, not today. What do you do when there is no magic in your touch, and magic is what you need to pick your lady up off the floor? A wise man calls on the Lord.

I can recall when the presence of the Lord began to manifest in our tragedy. He came like the Fred Astaire of healing. He stepped in like a better dancer who taps your shoulder at a prom and says, "May I?" With a noted degree of skill, grace, and gentle concern, He began to take long, gentle strides that eased her distress and released her smile that had been locked up in the vault of her tragic loss. He pressed His hand into the small of her back and released her tension in a way that I could never do. After all, who else but He could touch the damaged tendons of her heart and heal the torn ligaments of her soul? Little by little, I noticed a gleam return to her eyes and subtle changes, such as an occasional hum or a returned sense of humor. Each of these symptoms could only be attributed to the God who restores the soul.

It is no wonder that He can restore the soul, for He is the lover of the soul. He can mend the past, the present, and the future. He is the therapist who relieves trauma no matter how it was incurred. Perhaps you have been through a devastating moment. Maybe no one has been able to heal the damage and revitalize the depletion. Your pain might not have been through the loss of a parent. Some of you have lost children. Some have buried your sons or daughters who died untimely deaths because of AIDS or some other deadly disease. Sadly, some have watched the caskets of their little children lowered into the ground because of some insane drunk-driving accident or drive-by shooting.

Some of you are grieving over the death of a relationship. You don't even understand why it died; you are forced to accept something that you cannot explain. You have replayed the events as a jury reviews the evidence. Accept that your deliberation is after the fact and pointless. The chance to change the verdict is over. You were an eyewitness to the demise of your relationship, and with it went your friendship. There were moments of rage that bordered on hatred, and then there were the nights of loneliness and the crazed feeling of lust and longing for the lover who is supposed to be your enemy. The relationship pined away like a sick person. It lost its vibrancy, then its excitement, until one day you came home and found out it had lost its commitment. Some of you have seen adultery. It is the saboteur of trust and the executioner of bonding. Some of you have walked into a room and seen an incident that was so shocking you relive it over and over again. It is one thing to be suspicious, and it is quite another to have a memory to contend with for the rest of your life. You dream about it and wake up in tears. It reruns before you like an old B movie that you have seen too many times before. I know that some of you are grieving over these relationships that crumbled before your eyes.

Perhaps you have been haunted by one of these issues or some other crisis. Have you known what it was like to want someone to rescue you from the pain? Well, my sister, let me save you some precious time. Only the Lord can heal deep pain. It does not matter whether your pain comes from a brutal rape kept secret, a fractured promise never fulfilled, or some other gut-wrenching disturbance. He is the prince of peace and He rides into the worst situations on the wings of hope. His divine hand over you gives sense to the tragic events that seemed meaningless. He knows how to orchestrate your pain and somehow bring a blessing out of a mess.

> For the brokenness of the daughter of my people I am broken; I mourn, dismay has taken hold of me. Is there no balm in Gilead? Is there no physician there? Why then has not the health of the daughter of my people been restored?　　　　Jer. 8:21–22 (NAS)

I share my failure to help my wife through her mother's death, so through it you might find success. It represents men's failure to reach an expectation that we set or our ladies set that is lofty and unrealistic. Often, when we can't reach this expectation, we cover up the guilt with anger. Women get angry because we are not living up to their expectations. But the truth is the lady is looking for the Lord in her lover, and He is not there. If he is not God and cannot really erase the tragedies of your darkest hour, would you settle for a man who just wants to hold your hand through a night?

There is no need to mask the truth. Men are not God. Men cannot restore what life has stolen. My carefully contrived words of sympathy seemed hollow compared to His merciful presence. He was the healing balm that began to restore my wife's soul. His anointing was the sedative that numbed the aching hurts and gave her soul a chance to heal itself. I was glad to see Him intervene and I was humbled to recognize what a gulf there is between what a man can do and what the Lord can do. I shudder to think what women do who face trauma without Him. Are they left to look for healing in themselves? Is the lady able to heal herself? The answer is a miserable no. You may have become so self-reliant that you are not God-reliant. Your attempt to avoid the disappointment of rejection has created self-idolatry. In short, you depend on yourself for everything. You have become your own lover and your own Lord. But you are no better at it than men are. Let the Lord be God in your life. If He could restore my wife's wilted soul, He can restore yours as well. But you must seek the Lord; you can't play God. I know you may be independent, but you need to allow God to help you through the night. He alone can mend you. You cannot do this on your own.

Yes, only God can truly heal. Unfortunately, some women still frantically pursue relationships in the hopes that someone somewhere will stop the pains of life. They become prostitutes. They do anything for love or attention. Their past becomes the pimp; it demands of them, and they respond. They are trapped in the dungeon of desperation and degradation. They will sell themselves. No, it is not for money that they become involved with undesirable men; it is for a few minutes of feeling special to combat the multiple months of feeling like "no big deal!" They go through men like old ladies rummaging through the discount rack at a one-day sale. They are searching through trashy relationships and affairs looking for a morsel of love or a cup of affection. These women are not like the ones who think they can handle everything on their own. These girls know that they can't handle it on their own. But they have been convinced that somewhere there is a man sitting on a white horse who will finally show up and wake them out of this nightmare of a life they have had to live.

From fairy tales to psychic phone line commercials, we perpetuate a myth that says there is a "Mister Right" out there who can make your life wonderful. I have counseled countless women who think that all they need is companionship. How foolish for you to think that someone is going to ride in on a white horse with no needs of his own. Generally speaking, men today are looking for someone to answer their 911 call. Everyone is looking for a savior, but they are looking in the wrong places and the marriages are coming apart at the seams. Do you really think that a man is going to come looking for the kind of weight your healing would place upon him? Even if he were willing (and most men are not), is he able? Of course not. Life is not that simple.

Eros love is no replacement for Godly love. Human love is far overrated in our society. It has been used for everything from a cure for depression to a way to sell toothpaste. We are bombarded with television commercials that suggest if you use this breath mint, men will chase you down in the streets and meet your every need. He can no more meet your every need than the breath mints can make him chase you, but subtly we have bought into this whole idea of commercialized, fast-food love. But love is not an aspirin that you take at night and it makes you get up refreshed in the morning. Love is not the cure. Many times it is the cause of the pain. It hurts to love, for we are never hurt by those we care nothing about. No investment means that there is no potential for loss. So should we avoid love? No, absolutely not. But we need to put love in the right perspective. Many relationships would be healed of the terrible disappointment if both parties would stop expecting the other to be an antibiotic for the infections of life. I can imagine by now you are starting to say, "Oh, stop telling me what doesn't work and tell me what does work." Well, I'll say it again. Only God can heal what you have been trying to medicate. We can medicate the pain and camouflage the symptoms, but they will return. Real, complete healing comes only from the one who made the heart that is now broken. He can heal your broken heart.

Night Comes Before Light

Many have remained angry at someone for years for not curing them in a time of need. Foolishly, they are filled with bitter disappointment, saying, "You didn't stand by me. You were not there for me!" It may be true that you didn't get the support that you had a right to expect, but even if you had gotten what you think you needed, it would not have been enough to stitch the wound shut! Maybe God just bypassed the interns and brought in the head surgeon to heal you Himself. Accept that as a blessing and move on.

I want to speak on behalf of the men of the world. We can be your lovers, but we cannot be your Lord. It is not realistic for us to tell you that we can. We are in need of His assistance. We need healing ourselves. As much as we want to be your heroes, we cannot be your savior. Most of us live to impress you, and sometimes we are so desperate to impress you that we promise what we can't deliver. Sometimes your own sisters promote the myth of male power by suggesting that they have everything in their companion. They are so loyal to the myth of perfect relationships that they will never divulge the fact that there are some areas that no one touches in any of us. But those areas need to be touched, and that need drives you back to God.

Men are turning back to God as well. Never in the history of this country have we seen millions of men gathering in Washington seeking spirituality and renewal. I laughed as some of the press worked to assign some hidden agenda to the meeting of men who wanted only to pray. It was hard to write about it, because it was not a tangible need that brought those men together. Men are desperately needing to find God because life has shown us that we are not Him. Not only do we need to defer to Him with our pain and unresolved issues, there are times that we need to climb up in Daddy's arms and allow him to mend us as well. You cannot bear the responsibility for healing us, no more than we can heal you. We may be each other's nurses or assistants, but we cannot perform the surgery. We all are, at best, just helpers. We are only apprentices; the detailed craftsmanship must come from the Master.

Midnight Waltz

When my wife needed Him the most, when I needed Him the most, He took over the dance. I guess He was tired of watching me stumble over her feet and mishandle her recovery. I needed His help. She was too much for me alone. Men seldom admit that, but we should. It is a freeing experience to admit that we are not and cannot be everything. It is the Lord that fills in the blanks that we leave undone. He waltzed her in ways that I could never have done. His rhythm is consistent, His pitch is perfect, and He glides through without fear. A good woman will glide with God in such a flow that many men become intimidated by her relationship with God. But some of us are too relieved to be intimidated. We just want to see the lady whole and healed.

So to my sisters I say, step to the beat of God's healing rhythm and respond willingly as He glides you through the tragedies into the victories. Allow Him to waltz you through what others have clung to and release you into what He has prepared for you. It has been a long night. It has been laced with prayer and faith, and now, in the candlelight of His word, He has come to take you where men cannot journey. He will make you strong where we will not. He is the lover of your soul.

Every lady should have Him in her life. He is a necessity. If there has been something missing in your life, perhaps it might be His presence. If you have left Him out, sooner or later you will encounter moments that only He can handle. He is standing there with His ever-loving arms stretched out to you. His eyes are gleaming with a passionate concern. He knows so well what you need. His loving voice is pleading, "May I have this dance?"

Chapter Sixteen

On to the Morning!

Life is a series of challenges and tests. It comes fully equipped with pleasure and pain, sunshine and rain. It is a potpourri of every feeling imaginable. I have been in the storm, and the one thing I must tell you is that the storm does pass over after a while. The storm passes, the rain stops, the clouds recede, and the day breaks. What a blessing it is when the night has been long to know at last it is morning.

The Lord Himself gives us new days. I held my wife through the night, and she has held me. We are not perfect; we are just two crippled people who have made the commitment to hobble home together. It is so nice to know that I do not have to stumble back home on twisted limbs and broken knees alone. She and I have decided to walk all the way to the ground together, rain or shine, right or wrong, weak or strong. So what of the night? If it comes, it comes. It will have to pass over. When it passes, we will be safe in the arms of each other and of the one who watches us through the night.

God stopped her tears, but I got to wipe her eyes. Tomorrow she may have to wipe mine. But no matter, at least the lady has the lover and the lover has the Lord. We have Him for the moments that are too much for human minds to resolve. I was there to be a witness in the night, and I am here to tell you of the morning light. There is no better way to wake than to wake up with the sun drenching across the hopeful face of someone whose dark face has become the canvas for the bright rays of tomorrow.

If you are blessed to live a long life, you will see many triumphs and face many challenges. You will laugh gleefully, and you will wail in pain. You will experience every feeling known to man. You will see good times as well as bad. No one can escape bad times. No one is exempt. No one can shield or hide us from pain. These are realities that come to the richest homes as well as to the impoverished. Simply stated, this is life. It is the way it is. It has always been, and it will always be. Yet in the midst of the madness, when we are facing situations that seem to have no rhyme or reason, it helps to know that somewhere beyond the passions and pains there is a God.

> Blessed be God, even the Father of our Lord Jesus Christ, the Father of mercies and the God of all comfort; Who comforteth us in all our tribulation, that we may be able to comfort them which are in any trouble, by the comfort wherewith we ourselves are comforted of God.   II Cor. 1:3–4

One of the many names for the Lord is Comforter. I cannot tell you what an excellent description that is. He is the great comforter. His presence can make us comfortable in the most uncomfortable situations. He can unravel the dark shroud of grief and release the captive heart that is buried within. He skillfully and carefully pulls all of us out of things that we thought we could not get out of. He has the ability to wipe away trauma and restore peace. He catches our tears and collects our pains. He has the capacity to be there for you. Whenever you need Him, He is there.

All of us will live and love and experience loss before our time here is done. It is the loss of things that makes us appreciate what we still have. It is the bitter taste of poverty that makes prosperity so sweet. How can we celebrate triumph if we have not faced defeat? As the Word of God says, there is a time for everything. "A time to weep, a time to laugh; a time to mourn, and a time to dance" (Eccles. 3:4, KJV). And so it is, we live each day not knowing from moment to moment what we will have to face, not knowing what tomorrow holds. But it is a great comfort to know who holds tomorrow. Tomorrow is not in the hands of your supervisor, your children, your husband, or anyone else. Tomorrow is not yours to manipulate. It is not mine to dominate. Tomorrow is in the hands of the Lord. Whatever you do, take time to speak to Him because you will need Him before morning.

> . . . weeping may endure for a night,
> but joy cometh in the morning.
>
> Ps. 30:5

He will be there when husbands, lovers, children, friends, jobs, and money are gone. He is there in the night. He is there for the dark places—and we all have dark places. Now take courage, my sister, and understand that weeping may endure for a night, but joy cometh in the morning. It may seem that it has been a long night, but when the night is over, there will always be morning light. So you have had a long night and tossed and turned trying to find rest, but the night is far spent and the day is at hand; soon it will be morning.

Think about it. You've been knocked down to the ground, but you've always gotten up. No matter how dark the night, you've always lived to see the light. Understand that it is God's grace that has protected you and provided for you, brought you and secured you. Times change, seasons change, but not God. He is always the same. He is the same God who brought you through your past, and He promises you your future. Understand you will arise. Motivation to survive comes from the inner well that you possess within. The Lord is the source that fills that well. Let it flow. You don't have to make it flow, just let it flow.

Our children's prayer says it best. Little

children clad in flannel pajamas kneel down beside their beds, clasp their hands, close their eyes, and whisper the words of this simple prayer: "Now I lay me down to sleep, I pray the Lord my soul to keep." They say those words tenderly, preparing to rest through the night. If we could only keep those words alive as we grow older, there would be no trauma we could not survive. For in that simple phrase lies a deep and profound truth. The truth of the matter is that there are some things that we cannot control. There are some stages, ages, and places in life that all of us must face. When we face those places, we must lie down like children and rest like sheep, and trust the Great Shepherd to watch over us through the night. He will always be there, to see you through the night. So, whatever happens, do not be afraid, because you are never truly alone.

You are a woman of excellence. You are strong and powerful in your own right. Occasionally, if God so wills, He sends to an excellent woman an excellent husband who has the grace to be a lover and the anointing to be a friend. Occasionally, He sends someone to sing the songs that her heart longs to hear. Occasionally, He sends a strong arm to wrap around her feeble body and give her a moment of rest and tranquillity. But none of these experiences will ever take the place of the ultimate experience. For the greatest source of strength she will ever know is the moment she knows her Lord.

No matter what sorrow life has brought before you, don't stop until you see morning, because morning does come. It is at the end of every night. It is at the end of every broken home. It is at the end of every tragic divorce. But it does come. It is at the end of setbacks, betrayals, delays, and denials, but when it's all over, morning does come. I challenge you, my sister, my lover, my wife, my mother, my friend, hold out for the morning because it does come. Do not allow the tragedies of life to so depress you that you lose your expectation of the morning. Do not allow the bitter disappointments and losses you face to rob you of the expectations of daybreak. Wake up singing hallelujah in the morning. Breathe in fresh air, expel the stale air of your past, and say to yourself, "I can feel the breaking of day." And it will come. I encourage you to overcome obstacles with confidence. Survive traumas with triumph. I encourage you to find solace through sorrow and to know comfort in the midst of crises, because the morning does come.

Some years ago John Newton penned these words during a crisis in his own life. It is a hymn that strengthens the heart and rekindles the flame to survive. It has always encouraged my faith and motivated my spirit, and I know that it had to be divinely inspired. He says, "Through many dangers, toils and snares, I have already come. Twas grace that brought me safe thus far and grace will lead me on. Twas grace that taught my heart to fear and grace my fear relieves; how precious did that grace appear the hour I first believed." If you're not familiar with those verses you might remember this one: "Amazing Grace how sweet the sound that saved a wretch like me; I once was lost but now I'm found, was blind but now I see." Isn't that what morning is all about? Stepping out of blindness into seeing. It is my prayer that the darkness will roll back from every issue in your life like clouds being pushed from the sky by a strong gust of wind. The Lord can do that for you; He will bring you grace, He will help you see, and He will watch you through the night.

The only thing that He would ask of you is to acknowledge that it is His grace that brought you through. It is not enough to say thank you. You need to be thankful.

You need to have an attitude of gratitude. It is a deep, subtle conviction of appreciation. To be thankful is to acknowledge that life has been tempestuous, but God has been faithful, and when all is said and done, He is still worthy of the praise.

Prepare to hear the blaring sound of a trumpet being blown, shrilling in your ears announcing the breaking of day. You cannot wait until you see the light to prepare for the day, for midnight announces to the waiting soul that the night is turning and the day is coming. Midnight is the turning point of night. It is that time when the sun begins its ascension and the darkness of night progressively begins to fade into the brightness of expectation. Be prepared! The night is coming to a close and the day is before you. It is time for you to go out to meet your destiny.

> And at midnight there was a cry made, Behold, the bridegroom cometh; go ye out to meet him. Then all those virgins arose, and trimmed their lamps. And the foolish said unto the wise, Give us of your oil; for our lamps are gone out.   Matt. 25:6–8

It is my assignment to announce to you that the bridegroom cometh. Go you out to meet him. This is no time to be left lying in the bed of despair—no matter how long the night, no matter how dark it seems. Whatever you went through, it's over. It is the breaking of day, and the bridegroom cometh. Now, my sister, don't be foolish and allow life to deplete you and rob you of your oil. You need the oil of the Holy Spirit now more than ever, for now is the time for you to trim your lamp, gather yourself, organize your dreams, and go ye out to meet him. Some of you have been distracted by the cares of life, but now is the time for you to walk into the room and tell your husband, "Baby, I'm back." Go ye out to meet him. I know in the strict sense of the text, it refers to meeting Christ, but the verse illustrates meeting Christ by discussing a woman meeting her groom. Could it then be possible that the precious Holy Spirit might help a woman who has been shut off from her husband to be able finally to go out to meet him rather than wait for him?

Men like a woman who goes out to meet them halfway. But you couldn't go before. You were in too much pain. If you did go, it was for the wrong reason. You were looking for a healing. Now you can bring healing with you. Like the maidens of yesteryear who went out to meet the groom in the wee hours of the night, you must be prepared to establish this moment in your life as a new era with Christ at the helm. Rest in His promises. Rely on His strength. Bask in His presence and know that you are His chosen vessel. Meet Him. He is waiting to usher you out of your past into your future.

You have to know that something or someone is waiting on you on the other side of your test. Your children are waiting, and your family is waiting. Ladies, your husband is waiting to be the lover in your life. The Lord wouldn't have brought you through it if He didn't have something for you or someone waiting for you. God is your Lord, but He called man to be your lover. Don't make the mistake of becoming so spiritually intertwined with the Creator that you do not allow what He has created for you to have his rightful place in your life. If God wanted you all to Himself, he wouldn't have given you a husband to love. As Eve woke up in the morning and found that God had a man waiting for her, your Adam is waiting for you. He is stretched out like a strong man on a sandy beach, just waiting for you. Don't keep him waiting too long.

Starting today, when you arise out of the bed, look the day straight in the face and declare with all the strength you can muster, "This is the day that the Lord has made. I will rejoice and be glad in it." While it is true that only the Lord can take you through the night, I must tell you it's the man's job to meet you in the morning. If you are married to a man who loves you, understand that he is waiting. He gave up the dance so that God could heal as only He can do. But when the dance is over and the night is past, Adam still wants to see you. And God is not jealous. He created you to be together. He gave you as a gift to Adam. You are God's answer to Adam's prayer. Lady, it is an awesome joy to be the man who waits for you on the other side of your challenge. Just don't keep Adam waiting. Now that you are awake and the night is finally over, Adam is saying, "Hey, woman, I have been waiting for you. Come here!"

To the lady who survives the night, we men know that it was God who brought you through it. But it was us He was bringing you to. It is a sensation of rapture to be the lover who gets the first kiss of a woman who is awake. Are you awake? Please give your man a sign. If he waited through the night, don't delay your recovery. The Lord says to the lover, "It's okay now. I brought her through it. It's your turn to love her." Then Adam is afforded the unique privilege of being the one who breathes the heated words of passion gently into your ear. Listen to him. Hear his love.

What? You felt the heat of it but you couldn't quite hear what he said? I know it's hard to hear. Men seldom speak love in words. We speak love in glistening eyes. We speak it in heavy sighs and tender smiles. Let me interpret this moment so that you can hear what is being said. He just looked so deeply into your eyes that he saw the trembling in your soul. He brushed the hair out of your face, touched the nape of your neck, and breathed gently into your ear. He just said, "Hey, baby girl, wake up. It's morning!"

About the Author

Bishop T. D. Jakes is the author of several best-selling books. His weekly television broadcast *Get Ready with T. D. Jakes* airs on Trinity Broadcasting Network and Black Entertainment Television in this country, and in Europe and South Africa. The founder and pastor of the 16,000-member Potter's Field Church in Dallas, Texas, he lives with his wife, Serita and their five children in Dallas.

Look for these latest Walker Large Prints

Footprints
Margaret Fishback Powers

How To Handle Adversity
Charles Stanley

Just As I Am
Billy Graham

Keep a Quiet Heart
Elisabeth Elliot

A Layman Looks at the Lord's Prayer
W. Phillip Keller

Letters to My Grandchildren
Charlie W. Shedd

Readings for Meditation and Reflection
C. S. Lewis

Stories for the Heart
Alice Gray

Among the many other titles available are:

Abiding in Christ
Cynthia Heald

And the Angels Were Silent
Max Lucado

Apples of Gold
Jo Petty

The Best of Catherine Marshall
edited by Leonard LeSourd

The Blood
Benny Hinn

A Book of Angels
Sophy Burnham

Book of Hours
Elizabeth Yates

Breakfast with Billy Graham

Brush of an Angel's Wing
Charlie W. Shedd

Encourage Me
Charles Swindoll

15 Minutes Alone with God
Emilie Barnes

Finding God
Larry Crabb

Finding God in Unexpected Places
Philip Yancey

A Gathering of Hope
Helen Hayes

Getting Through the Night
Eugenia Price

God Came Near
Max Lucado

Golden Treasury of Psalms and Prayers
Edna Beilenson

Good Morning, Holy Spirit
Benny Hinn

The Grace Awakening
Charles Swindoll

The Greatest Salesman in the World
Og Mandino

The Greatest Story Ever Told
Fulton Oursler

The Guideposts Treasury of Christmas

Heaven: Your Real Home
Joni Eareckson Tada

The Hiding Place
Corrie ten Boom

Hinds' Feet on High Places
Hannah Hurnard

Hope and Faith for Tough Times
Robert Schuller

Hope for the Troubled Heart
Billy Graham

I Am with You Always
G. Scott Sparrow

I've Got to Talk to Somebody, God
Marjorie Holmes

The Jesus I Never Knew
Philip Yancey

The Joyful Journey
Clairmont, Johnson, Meberg, Swindoll

Killing Giants, Pulling Thorns
Charles R. Swindoll

The Knowledge of the Holy
A. W. Tozer

Laugh Again
Charles Swindoll

Lord, Teach Me to Pray
Kay Arthur

Mere Christianity
C. S. Lewis

More Than a Carpenter
Josh McDowell

No Wonder They Call Him the Savior
Max Lucado

On the Anvil
Max Lucado

A Path Through Suffering
Elisabeth Elliot

The Power of Positive Thinking
Norman Vincent Peale

Prayers and Promises for Every Day
Corrie ten Boom

The Pursuit of Holiness
Jerry Bridges